THE HERO'S TALE

The Hero's Tale

Narrators in the Early Modern Novel

David H. Lynn

Director of Publications
Council for Basic Education, Washington, DC

St. Martin's Press   New York

First published in the United States of America in 1989

Printed in Hong Kong

ISBN 0–312–01621–2

Library of Congress Cataloging-in/Publication Data
Lynn, David Hayden.
The hero's tale: narrators in the early modern novel/by David
H. Lynn.
p. cm.
Bibliography: p.
Includes index.
ISBN 0–312–01621–2: $29.95 (est.)
1. English fiction—20th century—History and criticism.
2. Heroes in literature. 3. Courage in literature. 4. Narration
(Rhetoric) 5. First person narrative. 6. Modernism (Literature)
7. Conrad, Joseph, 1857–1924—Characters—Heroes. 8. Ford, Ford
Madox, 1873–1939. Good soldier. 9. Fitzgerald, F. Scott (Francis
Scott), 1896–1940. Great Gatsby. 10. Hemingway, Ernest,
1899–1961. Sun also rises. I. Title.
PR888.H4L94   1989
823'.912'09352—dc19
                                                          88–826
                                                          CIP

For Janet Davis Lynn

Contents

Acknowledgements

This book, and I, owe a great debt to Professor Anthony Winner for inspiration, editing, support – and no little criticism. Professors Hoyt Duggan and Douglas Day were thoughtful and most helpful readers of the manuscript. Peter Taylor provided reason, friendship, and inspiration. For far more than this book I thank Wendy F. Singer.

The article 'Watching the Orchards Robbed' appeared in *Studies in the Novel*, vol XVI, no. 4 (1984) and a version of this is reprinted here, by permission of North Texas State University.

The author and publishers wish to thank the following who have kindly given permission for the use of copyright material: Charles Scribner's Sons, a division of Macmillan, Inc., and the Estate of F. Scott Fitzgerald, for the extracts from F. Scott Fitzgerald, *The Great Gatsby*, copyright 1925 Charles Scribner's Sons, copyright renewed 1953; Charles Scribner's Son's, a division of Macmillan, Inc., and the Executors of the Ernest Hemingway Estate, for the extracts from Ernest Hemingway, *The Sun Also Rises*, copyright 1926 Charles Scribner's Sons, copyright renewed 1954; Random House, Inc., and Janice Biala, for the extracts from Ford Madox Ford, *The Good Soldier*.

1

Heart of Darkness: Marlow's Heroic Cry

[F]or good or evil mine is the speech that cannot be silenced.[1]

Aboard the *Nellie*, dusk settling as the tide ebbs on the Thames estuary, Marlow sits apart from the small group of men with whom he shares 'the bond of the sea' (p. 52). To them he recounts the story of his adventures in the Congo and his meeting with the extraordinary Mr Kurtz. The journey has been long and Marlow has himself been changed; the man who speaks is not the same as when he first joined the colonial enterprise. Marlow treats this earlier self as a distinct character, one not at all privileged, but subjected to varied ironies, great and small, throughout the narrative. This Marlow of the central tale is no fool, however; when recognition becomes possible, the ironies of situation, event, character, and so on, do not escape him. What distinguishes him later as narrator is an ironic vision larger than any particular situation or mode, a sense of *general* irony[2] which acknowledges the fundamental paradoxes of the story, of his efforts on the *Nellie* to recount it, and of man's desire to act meaningfully in the 'flash of lightening' (p. 49) that is the duration of civilization.

With this narrator, whose irony undermines the last foundations of moral realism, Conrad transforms the traditional frame narrative in *Heart of Darkness* and *Lord Jim*, and explores what heroism can yet suffice in a world cut off from its roots of humanism and human solidarity. During the course of the central tale of *Heart of Darkness*, Marlow undergoes a moral education and so achieves the ironic perspective that will distinguish his role as narrator. This narrative irony, as well as the structural relation between Marlow and Kurtz, was to be a shaping influence on four other major novels of the century's first quarter: *Lord Jim*, *The Good Soldier*, *The Great Gatsby*, and *The Sun Also Rises*. These novels, which this study will address in turn, share more than formal characteristics; they manifest concerns central to the first generation of the modern novel in

1

English – of the collapse of traditional values, of the individual realizing a new character defined against rather than within his socio-historical environment, of the final impotence of romantic ideals in face of a hostile or indifferent universe.

By examining the structure, the narrative irony, and the relationship between narrator and romantic figure in each of these novels, their shared concerns and the dramatic influence of each on the next will become apparent. And thus regarding each novel within the larger context will lead us to a richer understanding of its own individual achievements.

Such nineteenth-century novels as *First Love, Wuthering Heights, The Scarlet Letter,* and *Moby Dick,* different as they are, share similar structures. Each is a frame narrative; that is, a characterized narrator tells a story that has a dramatic influence on his own experience. This 'central' tale comes to us bound within the frame of his understanding. The *context* of his narration is defined in turn by the norms of a traditional community. The values and judgments of that social world, often depicted as shallow and spiritually oppressive, help shape the frame and so circumscribe the central tale. Thus, the narrative frame may be seen as embodying the values of realism, while the central tale is singularly romantic. The extraordinary is perceived and to some extent shaped by the perspective of the work-a-day and ordinary.

The central tales of these novels concern romantic figures isolated from social definition because of youthful innocence, adulterous passion, or egoistic disdain. Bridging the chasm of sensibilities is the narrator: a Lockwood or Ishmael. Further, each narrator embodies a significant bridge across the two main traditions of nineteenth-century fiction, romanticism and moral realism. Though anchored by temperament, education, and sensibility in the settlement (and therefore limited in a way the romantic figure is not), the narrator possesses an imaginative sympathy for the hero's passions and naivete. Often the identification extends deeply enough that narrator and hero are 'secret sharers' or doubles of each other, their differences complementary, their likenesses unspoken. This is as true for narrators who remain at a distance, as in *First Love* and *The Scarlet Letter,* as for those close enough at hand to risk a share in their hero's fate, bobbing coffin-borne to the surface only at the last moment.

These narrators celebrate their romantic heroes – celebrate their capacity for belief, their unrestrained energy and force, most of all their ability to act despite the protestations of reason and all the world. Although *Fear and Trembling* is not what we conventionally identify as a novel, Kierkegaard creates a similar relationship between the narrator Johannes di Silentio and Abraham, and then analyses that relation at some length.

> [A]s God created man and woman, so too He fashioned the hero and the poet or orator. The poet cannot do what that other does, he can only admire, love and rejoice in the hero. Yet he too is happy, and not less so, for the hero is as it were his better nature, with which he is in love, rejoicing in the fact that this after all is not himself, that his love can be admiration. He is the genius of recollection, can do nothing except call to mind what has been done; he contributes nothing of his own, but is jealous of the intrusted treasure.[3]

Decisive action is rarely vouchsafed the narrator, for his bond to the social world lames him with the awareness of paradox. Enthralled though he may be with the innocent, explosive vitality of the hero, so vivid in contrast to the world of norms and boundaries and nay-sayers, the narrator recognizes as well the dangerous naivete and egoism of the Heathcliffes and Ahabs. The narrator mediates, therefore, seeking through his craft to translate something of the hero's life into the heart of the settlement, especially for those who listen and can understand.

For all the significant continuations of the tradition, the five novels to be discussed in this study mark a profound break as well. *Heart of Darkness, Lord Jim, The Good Soldier, The Great Gatsby*, and *The Sun Also Rises* are all frame narratives during which the values and ideals of the past century – capitalism, colonialism, liberal faith in Progress, and so on – are revealed as illusory and corrupt. They can no longer sustain the secure norms which shaped earlier narrative frames. The fates of such romantic heroes as Jim and Gatsby disengage their narrators from the shelter of socially defined character. They too are torn outside the boundaries of the traditional community.

As a result, the focus of these novels shifts to the experience of the narrators themselves. They undergo educations similar to that found in novels of moral realism, familiar in such works as *Wilhelm Meister, Pere Goriot*, and *Great Expectations*. Pip and Rastignac begin their trials and educations without mature *character* – outside of historical definition. They must earn their places in the socio-historical world of the nineteenth century, which provides a complex structure of meanings to nourish individual character. Marlow, on the other hand, as will John Dowell, Nick Carraway, and Jake Barnes, sets off *with* a clearly defined social character. He must generate a new one for himself only when the fabrications of the old world can no longer disguise the corruptions of its ideals, the contrary impulses within his own soul, or the eternal threat of a universe indifferent to all human endeavour. This new character is founded on the moral vision he has gained during the central tale. Each narrator comes to see, and thus to shape, the world in terms that we can call *general irony*. This perspective juxtaposes a faith in the enduring value of solidarity, labour, and art, against a radical scepticism aware of encroaching chaos. With the romantic hero destroyed by his own naive egoism in conflict with the barren social environment, each of these narrators, though himself partly lamed by the relativism of irony, assumes the role of hero and transforms it. The new moral dualism of scepticism and faith structures the tale he tells. That tale, in turn, is his heroic act, his attempt to translate his experience into language so that his audience will in some way share it and the moral education be passed on.

II

Only with the Marlow stories, 'Youth' (1898), *Heart of Darkness* (1899), and *Lord Jim* (1900), does Conrad cast heroism and the social world as irremediably in conflict. In *The Nigger of the 'Narcissus'* (1897), for example, one discovers an earlier vision – one certainly more hopeful and perhaps more innocent – of selfless heroism in the cause of human solidarity. It is worth discussing *The Nigger of the 'Narcissus'* in some detail for two reasons: it depicts a community whose values and integrity yet survive, a vision of innocence from which all the narrators of this study have in some sense fallen away and for which they long. And the dangers overcome by the *Narcissus* anticipate those more potent ones that will shatter communities and characters in the later novels, necessitating new forms of heroism. If Conrad never again creates such a hero as Singleton, this sailor's unquestioning devotion to duty, ship, and sea, remains always an ideal.

Singleton is not a romantic figure of the same breed as Ahab or Heathcliffe, Jim or Gatsby. Rather, he represents an opposite pole of romanticism. His particular virtues make him akin to heroes in the fiction of Walter Scott, men of little speech and noble deed, such as Rob Roy and Ivanhoe. They embody ideals such as fidelity, selflessness, and honour. These are not men who belong to the quotidian world, and Scott places them in remote history or equally remote Highland glens. Conrad's Singleton indeed seems curiously out of place surrounded by flawed mortals. Like Wordsworth's Leechgatherer, he is a solitary survivor of a simpler, nobler generation always receding to the horizon, leaving behind lesser men of pettiness and complexity. The oldest sailor aboard the *Narcissus*, for half a century Singleton has dedicated his life to 'the austere servitude of the sea'.[4] Nearly inarticulate, he speaks rarely and then with the unthinking resonance of an oracle: 'The wisdom of half a century spent in listening to the thunder of the waves had spoken unconsciously through his old lips' (p. 24), we are told. By drawing the distinction between a ship and the men aboard her, he alone anticipates, however unconsciously, the troubles ahead:

> Singleton didn't stir. A long while after he said, with unmoved face: – 'Ship! ... Ships are all right. It is the men in them!' (p. 24)

Singleton has no wish to set himself apart from the rest of the crew. Their shared life as a community earns its meaning in loving and battling the sea. Singleton's identity is firmly rooted to his role aboard the ship. When the *Narcissus* is in danger he never loses himself or abandons his post.

> Apart, far aft, and alone by the helm, old Singleton had deliberately tucked his white beard under the top button of his glistening coat. Swaying upon the din and tumult of the seas, with the whole battered length of the ship launched forward in a rolling rush before his steady old eyes, he stood rigidly still, forgotten by all, and with an attentive face. In front of his erect figure only the two arms moved crosswise with a swift and sudden readiness, to check or urge again the stir of circling spokes. He steered with care. (p.89)

The last sentence, simple and spare in Conrad's rhetoric, is also his highest tribute. In a world thus rightly ordered, the true heroic act reaffirms not the individual but the integrity of the social organism.

The self discovers fulfilment precisely in selfless endurance and commitment to duty.

Each ship generates its own identity, and the crew of each voyage its own character. Yet these belong to a larger fabric of beliefs and illusions that makes life endurable. As in any society, the simple and terrifying truths of life – most fundamentally, that each man knows he will die – are hidden within the intricacies of that social fabric, which assigns duties, responsibilities, and rituals. At some level every sailor on the *Narcissus* knows that, given the unceasing threat of the sea, any voyage may be his last. But what he knows in the abstract appears at the same time unreal, an impossibility. It fails to penetrate as a truth that might well incapacitate him with fear and despair. For he feels not only his own life sustaining him, but the greater life of the crew. The ship will survive and he with it. His labour reinforces this sense of security. And, as with Singleton, each sailor earns a measure of heroism by fulfilling his responsibility in sweat and danger.

Perhaps the most telling passage on this issue comes with the narrator's farewell, years later, to the memory of his shipmates. Although the *Narcissus* has nearly succumbed to storms off the African cape, Conrad's attention is here directed less at the hostile universe and its implications for an individual than at the community that must continue its struggle to survive from day to day.

> Haven't we, together and upon the immortal sea, wrung out a meaning from our sinful lives? Good-bye, brothers! You were a good crowd. As good a crowd as ever fisted with wild cries the beating canvas of a heavy foresail; or tossing aloft, invisible in the night, gave back yell for yell to a westerly gale.   (p. 173)

In the teeth of an environment that constantly threatens man's survival, let alone any need for personal significance, the crew has shared the sort of heroism and meaningfulness most manifest in Singleton. Yet we should note that the narrator's claim is oddly tentative, framed as a rhetorical question. This can be seen as one result of the sudden appearance of an 'I' at the novel's conclusion. The narrator has moved from the dispassionate recording of events in the third person, to the first-person plural, and here at last to existence as a flesh-and-blood character within the story and a narrating consciousness attempting to make sense of that story. In a sense he has grown, been educated, achieved character itself (anticipating Marlow's later moral educations). As Michael Levenson has suggested, this abruptly self-conscious narrator 'makes possible a sustained moral summary which guarantees appropriate depth of emotion and provides the coherence of an individual perspective'.[5] With consciousness, especially when bred out of the dangers of such a voyage, arises a measure of uncertainty: hence, the narrator's tentativeness.

If the narrator's self-consciousness surfaces only at the last, egoism has appeared earlier as the greatest of threats to the ship's solidarity. As in Marlow's solitary journey into the heart of darkness, the *Narcissus* faces danger not only from without, but from egoism, greed, and hypocrisy which can breed within a community. Having survived the sea's tempests, the ship's solidarity is sapped by human dissension. The great negro James Wait, a head taller than other men, shamming sickness to avoid work – all the while wasting in fact with consumption – shares with the sea-rat Donkin a selfishness and self-consciousness that alienate them from their traditional roles and nurture dissatisfaction among their shipmates.

Wait shams illness to hide, most especially from himself, the fact that he is being consumed from within, as if by his own egoism. He asserts himself with ceaseless demands, all the while never allowing the suspicion to disappear that he is tricking crew and officers – and hoping to cheat death itself. A *momento mori*, he dominates the consciousness of the crew. They willingly play at sustaining the lie which no one for long believes, save perhaps Wait himself. This living death's-head undermines finally that fundamental function of social ritual: the disguising of death as an immediate, inescapable reality. His egoism, his fear of death, nearly drive the crew to mutiny in their confusion and anguished primordial self-consciousness. Only the apparently instinctive understanding of the captain saves the *Narcissus* from chaos. Like Singleton, he is true to his role and stands in opposition to the dangerous egoism of Wait and Donkin. Such egoism, however, will exact a more terrible price in *Heart of Darkness* and *Lord Jim*.

III

As narrator of 'Youth', Marlow has not yet developed the sophistication or heightened self-awareness that characterizes his role in *Heart of Darkness*. The primary narrator, however – one of Marlow's immediate audience who later recounts the story himself – exercises a narrative irony that suspends the contrary sensibilities of Marlow as a boy and as an older man. The elder Marlow is so distant in temperament and perspective from his own youth that the innocence of the one is an absolute pole to the experience of the other. And of this Marlow himself seems unaware; it is the unnamed narrator who juxtaposes the two. That is, the narrative irony of the story establishes a rough equilibrium of perspective between innocence and experience. Seen in this way, 'Youth' represents a dramatic threshold for Conrad between *The Nigger of the 'Narcissus'*, in which community and heroic action can yet endure, threatened though they are, and *Heart of Darkness* and *Lord Jim*, where the meaningfulness of any human action becomes far more precarious.

Marlow's audience is initiated already into the secrets of the sea, yet unlike him they are men who now play social roles ashore. By role rather than name we know them – 'a director of companies, an accountant, a lawyer, Marlow, and myself'.[6] The last, *myself*, is in its way also an identification of role. For in keeping with what will later come to be labelled Impressionism, we find here a narrator insisting that he will recount – and in recounting unavoidably shape and interpret – his own experience of the story. The frame of Marlow's recalling a distant memory is thus itself enclosed within a larger frame. We are drawn by the narrator, already an initiate, into the privy circle and, because we are inclined by his reasonable, familiar tone to trust him, he shapes our expectations and responses, in essence creating a reader appropriate to the story.

Because we are drawn close to the primary narrator, our relation to Marlow is more distanced and controlled. His performance is itself a story, balanced by the one he tells. The correlation is crucial; our primary narrator presents the two tales, the two Marlows, young and old, juxtaposing them and insisting that the reader maintain his own detachment.

In form, 'Youth' follows one traditional pattern of frame narrative. As in Turgenev's *First Love*, an older man recollects an event of his youth which illustrates both the innocence of that distant time and how the event represented a rite of passage which led him away forever from innocence. Marlow recalls his first berth as second mate, aboard the *Judea*, an ancient ship of 400 tons, bound with a load of coal for Bangkok. With all of youth's hope and imagination the young Marlow is struck most by the romance of a faded gilt motto on her stern: 'Do or Die'.

Age-ridden, battered by sea and storms, the *Judea*'s fate is a prolonged death while attempting to do. At first glance the persistence of officers and crew in completing the voyage is heroic – it affirms the meaning of life at sea. As we have seen in *The Nigger of the 'Narcissus'*, throughout Conrad's career this remains the touchstone for the truest heroism: the self–abnegating devotion to duty that sustains the larger solidarity of a community and helps achieve its appointed task. At twenty, Marlow is already capable of momentarily stepping back with enough detachment to evaluate his own performance. And he finds it good; during the endless, exhausting pumping of the ship, it reassures his sense of fitness.

> And there was somewhere in me the thought: By Jove! this is the deuce of an adventure – something you read about; and it is my first voyage as second mate – and I am only twenty – and here I am lasting it out as well as any of these men, and keeping my chaps up to the mark. I was pleased. I would not have given up the experience for worlds.   (p. 12)

The self-conscious comparison with romantic adventure reinforces an important ironic function of the older Marlow's perspective – he never allows us to forget that the glory he conjured for himself as a boy was, at least in part, an illusion of youth.

Yet the tone of 'Youth' is hardly tragic; it is wistful rather than brooding. Marlow's apparent principal concern as narrator is to recapture a sense of the vitality, the hopes, the beliefs in courage and heroism of his youth, all the while reminding his audience that these were dreams soon faded. Young Marlow's eager pursuit of adventure seems at first glance only gently tempered. If we press it no further than this, Marlow's frame would serve, as in *First Love*, only to isolate an event from his youth that demonstrated his innocent vitality at the same time it determined his course into manhood.

The vision of the older Marlow is not simply jaded or disillusioned, however – the lessons of experience have quite transformed the world and man's capacity to act in it. As Marlow first addresses his

audience, and we among them, he provides an important gloss for
the tale to come.

> You fellows know there are those voyages that seem ordered for
> the illustration of life, that might stand for a symbol of existence.
> You fight, work, sweat, nearly kill yourself, sometimes do kill
> yourself, trying to accomplish something – and you can't. Not
> from any fault of yours. You simply can do nothing, neither
> great nor little – not a thing in the world – not even marry an old
> maid, or get a wretched 600-ton cargo of coal to its port of
> destination.   (pp. 3–4)

The implications of this passage should be striking: what does it
matter, finally, whether the *Judea*'s cargo of coal ever reaches
Bangkok? Such a question strikes deep at the heart of human
solidarity and of man's capacity to create a meaningful existence
for himself – what matter the tasks we set? The sea-rat Donkin
might have ventured this sort of anathema, but we would hardly
hear it from the lips of the captain of the *Narcissus*.

Now Marlow, as he pontificates in 'Youth', is clearly in his cups,
enjoying his own performance immensely. We should not lay too
great a burden on this one passage, for to do so would violate the
general tone and sense of the story. Nevertheless, behind the
apparently gentle ironies of 'Youth' lies a rather darker suggestion
of man's position in a world largely indifferent to his fate.

Marlow's perspective also involves a curious double standard as
he judges the characters of the story. By every means available,
Captain Beard struggles to complete the voyage, even after it is
clear the *Judea* is doomed. Coal dust explodes, blowing away much
of the deck, and still he seeks to do his duty, sending the crew aloft
to furl sails on masts that may plunge into the sea. This incident
prompts a bifurcated judgment; the crew follows their second
mate aloft on a needlessly dangerous exercise, and Marlow as
narrator launches into immediate praise of the British soul: 'That
crew of Liverpool hardcases had in them the right stuff' (p. 25).
Captain Beard, however, is dealt with more harshly, though he too
is committed to fulfilling his responsibility. We find the repeated
suggestion that the captain has been deranged by the ill fortune of
his first command.

The old man seemed excited. 'We will do it yet,' he said to Mahon, fiercely. He shook his fist at the sky. Nobody else said a word.   (p. 27)

Whereas the motto 'Do or Die' provides a standard for the crew to display its heroism, Marlow suggests that the captain, a man of experience, should be no victim of romantic innocence and that, aware of the indifference of a universe in which he 'can do nothing', he should more quickly abandon the effort and salvage what he can without further endangering his crew.

The ironic detachment of the *primary* narrator mediates between this latter-day scepticism and the hot-blooded illusions of the young Marlow. The man who listens to Marlow's tale and later recounts it from a more distant perspective establishes a fragile equilibrium between innocence and experience which, in turn, controls the wistful rather than brooding tone. This primary narrator mediates so that the reader never fully embraces either Marlow, young or old.

Despite the fire's final victory in sinking the *Judea*, 'Youth' is not at all a sad tale. Marlow sets off in a small boat for the last stretch of his journey into the East. A preparatory rite, it again tests his endurance and forces him to confront the rigours of a first command and of the sea. He responds not with a new sober estimate of man's limitations, but with fresh certainty of his own worth – a last glorious flowering of his innocence. The darker vision is supplied only in retrospect years later.

I remember the heat, the deluge of rain-squalls that kept us baling for dear life (but filled our water-cask), and I remember sixteen hours on end with a mouth dry as a cinder and a steering-oar over the stern to keep my first command head on to a breaking sea. I did not know how good a man I was till then. I remember the drawn faces, the dejected figures of my two men, and I remember my youth and the feeling that will never come back any more – the feeling that I could last for ever, outlast the sea, the earth, and all men; the deceitful feeling that lures us on to joys, to perils, to love, to vain effort – to death; the triumphant conviction of strength, the heat of life in the handful of dust, the glow in the heart that with every year grows dim, grows cold, grows small, and expires – and expires, too soon, too soon – before life itself.   (pp. 36–7)

Yet if the later vision tempers the exuberant illusions of youth, it does not negate them; the two story-times – the journey of the *Judea*, and the telling of the tale – kept distinct by the mediation of the primary narrator, define each other. Irony suspends them and strikes the resonance of each to each. And narrative irony suspends their two apparently paradoxical sensibilities, of infinite hope and of the recognition of human frailty, so that both remain potent, if qualified. Because of the boy's capacity to believe in them, the dreams of youth conquer, in their way and for a little while, the harsh realities of survival at sea. The frame of 'Youth' recalls the human truth of those illusions and of the capacity to believe; at the same time, however, it reinforces our awareness that they are lost to us, and we isolated, cut off from them by darker truths of experience.

IV

The initial stage of Marlow's education in *Heart of Darkness* follows his discovery that many of European society's values are corrupt; all the lip-service paid to colonial enlightenment conceals a limitless, savage appetite for profit. Awakening to these facts threatens his secure sense of identity and weakens him to dangers from without and within. Just as the sea and human egoism imperil communal harmony aboard the *Narcissus*, Marlow's character is undermined both by the wilderness and by his own atavistic instincts. And because the cultural foundations of his character, which would have buttressed it, have already been thoroughly discredited, to face down these dangers Marlow must discover a new moral ground. This achievement, as well as surviving what destroyed Kurtz, is surely heroic. But Marlow's true heroism, what marks his transformation of the role of romantic hero into something distinctively modern, is the act that insists on meaning within a universe scorning all meaning, the telling of the tale.

Marlow sets off for the Congo in the spirit of empirical adventure: that which remains unknown *can* be known, explored, conquered. And, according to this ideal, the quest is good, even heroic. The Stanleys and the Cooks bear with them civilization's sacred flame, and return with *knowledge*, as precious as ivory and jewels. Although Marlow's desire is, of course, not so grand, his impulse mirrors this sort of cultural fable.

In seeking a position as steamboat captain on the Congo, Marlow intends to penetrate the mysterious unmapped area that has intrigued him since childhood. He believes that the map may yet be filled in more fully, and that there exists a clear relation between its lines, colours, tags, on the one hand, and the physical world on the other. (For a sailor such trust must be absolute.) He accepts the arbitrary premises behind the function of a map just as he accepts the notion that to explore will bring him knowledge, and that to explore while working for the colonial company is natural if not noble. These beliefs, on which he has founded his life as a sailor, suggest his relative innocence as he begins his journey. He will come to see that the snake-like representation of the river is but a faint shadow of reality. Indeed, the map's failure of adequate description parallels his own later as narrator to describe the intense 'life-sensation' of his experiences.

The absurdity of the colonial enterprise – and of Marlow's conventional assumptions – manifests itself soon after he is aboard the French steamer bound for Africa. As it makes its way from port it comes upon a man-of-war anchored off the African coast, shelling the impassive bush.

In the empty immensity of earth, sky and water, there she was, incomprehensible, firing into a continent. Pop, would go one of the six-inch guns; a small flame would dart and vanish, a little white smoke would disappear, a tiny projectile would give a feeble screech – and nothing happened. Nothing could happen.

(pp. 61–2)

Such absurdity undermines any notion of individual significance. While three men a day die aboard the man-of-war, a steamer faithfully delivers their mail. Custom-house clerks are flung off at each stop along the way, some drowning in the surf before reaching their new posts. And later, in the midst of dying black men scattered at the periphery of the Company's Main Station, Marlow spies one with 'a bit of white worsted around his neck' (p. 67). Its significance Marlow can only wonder at, but the rag's mute gesture of the boy's individuality magnifies the already considerable horror.

An encounter with the absurd, akin to irony, strips away the assumptions of everyday life, the thoughtless habits and patterns by which we establish our identities, binding day to day. Marlow's sensibilities are assaulted by the chaos and arbitrary death about him. In stark contrast appears the chief accountant, a man whose substance is little more than the trappings of habit and social station. His dress is immaculate, his shirts flawless; the records he keeps are perfect, however distant their relation to the general disorder. A white agent of the Company lies dying in his office, black men expire on all sides, and the accountant emerges for a breath of air carrying a 'green-lined parasol' (p. 67) to protect him from the sun. In one aspect the parasol is a metonym, a single detail representing the true substance of the man. A metaphor as well, it is a prop of civilized man's acculturation. Like the bit of white rag about the black man's throat, the parasol is a statement of identity, declaring not only the accountant's individuality (what he may have of it), but the social context within which his identity can survive. In this way the parasol does in fact protect him; Marlow claims that here is an achievement of character, for the accountant's character resides securely in the externals of culture. He is impervious to the atrophy of values that so threatens Marlow.

For Kierkegaard in the nineteenth century as for Sartre in the twentieth, an immersion in the absurd, with its terror and disorientation, is necessary before man can be aware of the potential of his own freedom and, with that awareness always before him, generate a new identity beyond social definition. Those same elements of culture and of character that cloak the absurdity of our lives are shared fictions which, again for both Kierkegaard and Sartre, enslave men. Conrad, however, is never as sanguine as they in rejecting entirely the meaning bred within community, though no social world in his later fiction is again as secure as that of the *Narcissus*. As in *Nostromo*, the creation of community – of shared social values – remains always a higher goal than the isolated, if free, individual. Marlow's heroism in *Heart of Darkness* is equally fulfilled only with the act that seeks to translate individual enlightenment into new bonds of fellowship.

Nevertheless, Marlow's passage is similar to that of Kierkegaard's Knight of Faith or Sartre's Rocquentin. Again and again the absurdity of life in the Congo threatens his sense of self. Everywhere he turns, man's efforts appear ludicrous or corrupt. Identity must express itself in deeds, and to be robbed of the ability to act threatens that identity. A hero is needed for the task, and Marlow turns initially to Kurtz; indeed, he creates Kurtz as a romantic hero who will challenge both settlement and jungle.

While still at the Company's Main Station, Marlow encounters the legend of a 'very remarkable person' who 'sends in as much ivory as all the others put together' (p. 60). The chief accountant assures him that Kurtz 'will be a somebody in the Administration before long. They, above – the Council in Europe, you know – mean him to be' (p. 70). Although an agent for the Company which Marlow, himself its employee, has already recognized as morally bankrupt, Kurtz is apparently exceptional in other ways than merely the collection of ivory.

During the course of the months of travel and travail it takes Marlow to reach the Inner Station, he gathers further testimony from various sources. All indications are that Kurtz has crystallized one of the fondest dreams of the Victorian imagination. He has transformed economic materialism into a romantic ideal, and then come full circle, translating that ideal into his actions in the material world. In the Congo, Kurtz apparently intends to demonstrate that 'the Benthamite, utilitarian, and imperialist modes of thought turn out to be, not contraries, but the complements of Romantic individualism'.[7] Kurtz, thus intuited, represents the same cultural values shaken by Marlow's early experience. He is a bulwark in Marlow's imagination to the foundations of civilization, and his actions – though as yet vague and unspecific – must surely stand, Marlow believes, in opposition to the absurd hubris of the French man-of-war and to the sordid examples of other Company agents.

Garnering strands of information, legend, and conjecture, Marlow weaves a Kurtz. Although the relation to the flesh-and-blood man he eventually meets is tenuous, the construct is vivid enough, even heroic enough, so that Marlow aligns himself with it by a lie.

The first-class agent of the Central Station, a conspiratorial fellow himself, assumes that Kurtz and Marlow are in league to snatch away the security of his position and that of his crony, the Manager. Given the methods of the trade, such an inference is hardly far-fetched. When Marlow grasps the other's suspicions he nearly laughs. Yet the two of them, Marlow and the agent, are engaged in the same struggle of interpreting the mysterious motives of other men. And the reader's response should be to note the tentative nature of all such interpretations – for Conrad's art insists that we engage in a very similar task.

To separate himself from the moral stench of the Central Station as well as to 'be of help to that Kurtz' (p. 82), Marlow lies, in essence, by not rejecting the agent's surmise. As throughout *Heart of Darkness*, however, irony undercuts the best of intentions. Regardless of motive all actions become equivocal. By attempting to repudiate corruption with a lie, Marlow becomes 'in an instant as much of a pretence as the rest of the bewitched pilgrims' (p. 82). He is caught in a dilemma that foreshadows Kurtz's greater failure: the translation into action of a moral idea, here the vague desire to aid Kurtz's 'mission', risks tainting that idea. Emilia Gould in *Nostromo* must come to terms with this same realization: 'There was something inherent in the necessities of successful action which carried with it the moral degradation of the idea.'[8]

Of course, Kurtz himself is still no more than an idea for Marlow –a word, a name, around which he has woven all the elements of the 'human context'.[9] Personal history, deeds done, assumed beliefs and values, contribute to this fiction, and Marlow has imaginatively created the substantial framework, all the trappings of character – not so very different from the accountant's parasol –while the centre remains an enigma. All the reality of a Kurtz exists without Kurtz. Yet we believe that Marlow's creation (and our own to the extent we participate in the interpretive process) bears a valid relation to the man who has come to the Congo.

The first troubling suspicion, however, that Marlow's expectations of Kurtz may be flawed – and Kurtz flawed too – dawns on him while overhearing the Manager. A great load of ivory has arrived from the Inner Station, delivered by Kurtz's assistant. Apparently intending to return to civilization, Kurtz travelled three-hundred miles of the way himself, only to wheel about suddenly and retreat up the river. The Manager is 'astounded at anybody attempting such a thing'. He is 'at a loss for an adequate motive' (p. 90).

Marlow too, of course, is in the dark. But he faces another interpretive dilemma: what to make of a perfectly clear action conjoined with a mysterious motive? The enigma blossoms into an image – Kurtz is suddenly more than a word.

I seemed to see Kurtz for the first time. It was a distinct glimpse: the dugout, four paddling savages, and the lone white man turning his back suddenly on the headquarters, on relief, on thoughts of home – perhaps; setting his face towards the depths of the wilderness, towards his empty and desolate station. I did not know the motive. Perhaps he was just simply a fine fellow who stuck to his work for its own sake. (p. 90)

The last suggestion, of Kurtz's loyalty to his work, puts the best face on the matter; it would be high praise to his steadfastness, setting him akin to Singleton, did we not sense a shift in Marlow's tone. Even as he presents in the simplest language a possible motive for Kurtz's return up river, as if to approximate his own innocence while at the Central Station, we realize that the flatness of tone – fine fellow – may well hint at an ironic, covert meaning. The inscrutable image of Kurtz and his paddlers disappearing into the wilderness, set against the pat surmise that he is dedicated to his task, creates a sense of disjunction and further absurdity. That no clear alternative possibility suggests itself, however, deepens the mystery. If not for his work, why? At the same moment that Marlow first imaginatively glimpses an image of the man with whom he has aligned himself, Kurtz becomes more incomprehensible than ever.

By using irony in this way, Marlow calls attention to himself as narrator; the central tale recedes as audience and reader are compelled to step back and interpret for themselves. This is only one of the many instances in the novel when we are reminded of the two narrative frames, Marlow's and the primary narrator's. Usually the process is overt as Marlow skips back and forth in his discourse across the events of the story, and from the story-time of the journey to the story-time of its telling. With each leap back to the *Nellie* we become aware once more that Marlow's tale exists within another frame, established by the primary narrator, as in 'Youth'.

The primary narrator's role is rather diminished in *Heart of Darkness*, however. Where the Marlow of 'Youth' had an ironic perspective only on his own younger days, as narrator of *Heart of Darkness* he has achieved a broader and more complex ironic vision, including a detachment from himself as he speaks. The principal function of the primary narrator is to establish once again a distance between the reader and Marlow, underscoring the irony of the immediate situation – that the story can never recreate the full intensity of the experience – and allowing the reader to decide for himself to what extent Marlow succeeds in the effort, to what extent he fails. Yet the primary narrator here is *not* properly an ironist; he does not intend that Marlow reveal himself as an innocent victim. He observes, without explicit or implied judgment, the inescapable irony of Marlow's attempt to communicate in his tale what words alone cannot suffice to express.

Marlow openly declares his own frustration, both what he felt while at the Central Station attempting to fathom the reality of Kurtz, and equally at language's incapacity to recreate the intensity of life. 'I did not see the man in the name any more than you do', he claims. 'Do you see him? Do you see the story? Do you see anything?' (p. 82)

Part of the burden of communication is hereby shifted to his audience; the effort must be shared, each reader coming to terms with the story in his own way. Although the reader is thus initially isolated, new community arises as well. As ironist, Marlow invites the insightful participant to join him in dismissing the 'surface' meaning of his language and in sharing the silent search for alternative possibilities.[10] The creation of a fellowship of initiates whose vision of the world has been transformed thus becomes a central goal of Marlow's narrative struggle in *Heart of Darkness*. The values and assumptions of this fellowship will in turn help fashion Marlow's own new character.

Yet while one function of the irony generates solidarity, Marlow's awareness of his own limitations reinforces his anguish about whether he can ever adequately communicate the life-sensation of his story. He realizes that 'what happened or what is will never fully yield to language and the ordering faculties of the mind'.[11] The telling of the tale can work towards understanding, towards re-establishing significant contact between isolated people; yet Marlow's perception of his own, and language's, shortcomings also undermines any such renewed brotherhood.

While still at the Central Station, Marlow continues to interpret the world in terms of the culturally defined identity already slipping away from him. Events beyond the pale of normal experience remain alien and mysterious. Kurtz's withdrawal into the wilderness jars the Manager's equanimity and Marlow's imagination because both readily recognize the menace surrounding the settlement. The motive Marlow has suggested – Kurtz's loyalty to his work – is further shaken by its incongruity with the actual deed.

There is a considerable breach between Kurtz's retreat into the wilderness and any suggested motive of continuing with a task that has already been overwhelmingly successful. Knowing what he already does of the fevers and savagery that lie up the river, Marlow's imagination can not yet assimilate possibilities that dwell beyond common expectations.

As Marlow continues his journey he in fact encounters *two* wildernesses: the primeval universe of jungle and river, and the unrestrained desires of man's own id, his pre-civilized heart of darkness. The customs of sea-life and of his socialized character have protected him from nakedly confronting these perils before. But on the Congo, snags in the river and fever threaten every moment, while the wild dances of primitive tribes stir more internal dangers. These realms are far from identical. They mark poles of normal experience. Yet Marlow ventures entirely beyond the normal. As his character slowly disintegrates – though never to the point of extinction – the wildernesses, external and internal, converge.

Stripped of the husk of civilization's saving illusions, Marlow clings to the quick of character by repairing the steamer and keeping her afloat. Although the illusions and hypocrisy of European society are exposed, Marlow never abjures what may be seen as its older, more fundamental sources of value. These make up a starker, simpler code, similar to that of Singleton and the captain of the *Narcissus*. This code of human behaviour sustains the hearts of both the individual and his community. Labour, as one of its elemental principles, possesses always for Conrad a redeeming virtue; through dedication to it a man can discover 'his own true stuff ... his own inborn strength' (p. 97). The grimy beetle with her crew of cannibals and her corrupt pilgrims survives because of Marlow's determination, as the *Narcissus* did thanks to Singleton's. Much of Marlow's character has been torn from him, but labour, with its direct relation to the small community for which he is responsible, provides an immediate structure to which he can attach himself and face down the call of the savage.

Labour also exemplifies a threshold that determines limits of concourse between demands of the external world and demands of the self. The business of piloting the steamer along treacherous waters is not only a social chore that provides identity for Marlow, but a means by which he defines himself, marking off a boundary between self and a hostile world. His labour is the objectification of a man's 'own true stuff' and of the restraint by which he delimits himself.

Marlow's duties take on an unreal quality, however, as he draws closer to Kurtz and the Inner Station. Neither his skill nor his dedication will determine the boat's fate; it is at the mercy of a random wilderness. Any action, even speech, directed out into the world comes to seem pointless.

> I fretted and fumed and took to arguing with myself whether or no I would talk openly with Kurtz; but before I could come to any conclusion it occurred to me that my speech or my silence, indeed any action of mine, would be a mere futility.   (p. 100)

For Marlow the loss of speech represents the nearly total loss of self. His recovery – a rebirth to a new, self-defined character – will culminate in the heroic cry I have used as an epigraph: that his is the voice, as witness, seer, narrator, that 'cannot be silenced'. As he speaks, Marlow's tale is a continuing insistence on meaningful survival.

By the time Marlow arrives at the Inner Station, fearing that Kurtz is dead, the reader already knows much of what he is to discover. As narrator Marlow is more concerned with our recognition of the dramatic irony of events – so that we remain detached and interpreting – than with the sustaining of suspense. To this end, the narrative has returned over and over again to the *Nellie*, preparing Marlow's audience. While describing the attack of Kurtz's savages on the steamer and the loss of his black helmsman, Marlow draws back to the frame narrative and reveals some of the truths he was yet to encounter.

> And the lofty frontal bone of Mr. Kurtz! They say the hair goes on growing sometimes, but this – ah – specimen, was impressively bald. The wilderness had patted him on the head, and, behold, it was like a ball – an ivory ball; it had caressed him, and – lo! – he had withered; it had taken him, loved him, embraced him, got into his veins, consumed his flesh, and sealed his soul to its own by the inconceivable ceremonies of some devilish initiation.
>   (p. 115)

With privileged knowledge we watch as the steamer docks at the Inner Station. Through his binoculars Marlow studies the ruined settlement. All that remains of a fence or enclosure is 'half-a-dozen slim posts ... in a row, roughly trimmed, and with their upper ends ornamented with round carved balls' (p. 121). As so often, Marlow's interpretation is stymied – information that seems straightforward, such as these ornamented stakes, and which he therefore interprets according to reasonable expectations, reveals itself as alien to such expectations.

A fence physically establishes boundary, defines by limitation; its token remnants are reassuring to Marlow if only as symbolically demarcating the ruined settlement from the jungle. Like his own labour, the fence is an apparent objectification of the human spirit defining itself. The dramatic irony is intense, of course, for the reader has recognized that the two wildernesses have already triumphed here. The poles symbolize not restraint but complete abandon. No fence, no restraint has any place in this settlement – on top of the stakes sit the heads of Kurtz's enemies.

Kurtz's labour has never aimed at self-definition through discipline, but at self-exaltation. If discipline requires a certain selflessness in order to give boundary to the self, Kurtz denies any such boundary, projecting himself into the world, like Wait and Donkin aboard the *Narcissus*, through language and eloquence. We learn that his writing is 'high strung' (p. 117) and, according to a journalist who once knew him, that he 'couldn't write a bit' (p. 154). Yet the sound of his voice, its musical cadence rather than the precise rhetoric of his words, has moved people to find in him an intensification of their own ideal self-images and values. This is as true of the Manager of the Central Station as of Kurtz's Intended who, a year after his death, claims that 'he drew men towards him by what was best in them' (p. 159). Why else would the Manager and his gang of thieves so fear Kurtz if they did not believe that he was, in the name of virtue, beating them at their own game? In their turn, the tribes of the Congo adore Kurtz for the depths of savagery they spy in him, not just for the thunder and lightning of his guns.

While surrounded by the defining context of late nineteenth-century European culture, Kurtz was able to feed the enormous demands of his ego within socially recognized limits. By representing the epitome of liberal and capitalistic ideals, Kurtz's own individuality was celebrated. As long as European culture provided structure and restraint, Kurtz could be, superficially, the most civilized of creatures. However, when he arrives in the wilderness to prove that the ideals of humanitarianism and colonialism can be wed – by such a hero as himself, binding contraries by the force of his romantic will – social restraint disappears and his character disintegrates. The jungle offers temptation and pleasure, not boundary. And Kurtz lacks the true stuff of character founded on social values as well as on individual ego. He is hollow. Like other romantic figures, he is a 'potentially divided self',[12] torn by contradictory impulses and a voracious egoism. In the wilderness Kurtz's integrity collapses; only the extremes of appetite and intellect, of savagery and idealism survive.

Once again Marlow must choose, but now between the reality of Kurtz's failure and the Manager's 'moral judgment' in the name of society: no longer a choice between virtue and vice, but between 'nightmares' (p. 138). He is disabused of innocence, aware of corruption everywhere, yet he chooses Kurtz once more. For Kurtz is as honest in his way as the wilderness, which does not dissemble its darkness, its threat to man, or its indifference to his fate. Kurtz's continued preaching of humanist ideals may be followed immediately by memories of savage self-indulgence – both possess a mad honesty in contrast to the Manager's enduring hypocrisy.

Marlow's choice poses a further threat to his identity, however. He risks losing himself entirely in what Kierkegaard calls the 'infinite absolute negativity' of irony.[13] This is a fundamental danger in being forced to choose between nightmares. As irony undermines the foundations of certainty, all meaning, value, character, may slip away, may become as impenetrable as the wilderness. Sophia Antonovna in *Under Western Eyes* warns of the dangers of irony, which destroys any simple and absolute faiths.

> Remember, Razumov, that women, children, and revolutionists hate irony, which is the negation of all saving instincts, of all faith, of all devotion, of all action.[14]

The menace of such absolute negative irony stripping away *all* meaning and value is the final assailant on Marlow's character. His choice to remain loyal to Kurtz is, at this stage, hardly a moral affirmation. Thus, he is his own threat – his education has flung him this far, but he must yet reach beyond an isolating radical irony.

During the night that the steamer lies docked at the Inner Station, Kurtz crawls from his cabin and towards the camp fires of his savage followers. The scene echoes his return up the river a year earlier. Marlow plunges into the forest after him. Having chosen this nightmare, the battle is with himself and for himself, as much as with Kurtz. He imagines being stranded here, living alone and unarmed, 'estranged from existence', and lost irrevocably. But unlike Kurtz he clings to his duty to return and to defeat this dark side of his own soul by bringing 'the devil back to the security of the steamboat, [making] the shadow submit to the orderly world of civilization'.[15] Marlow binds himself to Kurtz so that he can then define himself as separate. He triumphs where Kurtz failed, by giving himself up to the darkness, but not losing himself in it. Once more his own true stuff – the personal code he has discovered within himself – saves him. It tempers the dangerous relativity of irony. This code of basic human values will form one pole in Marlow's new moral perspective of *general* rather than absolute negative irony. It will be balanced but never entirely overwhelmed by a radical scepticism towards all human aspirations. From the battle in the forest with Kurtz emerges, raw and tentative at first, the heroic character Marlow will bear as narrator.

Kurtz's failure, however, is of more immediate concern than Marlow's victory. In the tradition of Manfred and Heathcliffe, Kurtz's uncowering confrontation with fate and with the terrible truths of his own flawed soul – leading finally to an egoistic self-immolation – is more compelling than the preservation of the social self. In saving himself, Marlow has forgone following the path of romantic heroism to its fulfilment: the trail he blazes is less terrible, less glorious perhaps. Further, like the other narrators of this study, Marlow is somewhat lamed by his experience. His peculiarly modern heroism, founded on the perception of irony penetrating all of man's efforts, involves a loss of the unrestrained vigour typical of the romantic figure.

As the boat slips downstream towards his death, Kurtz raves of what is his due from the two worlds, savage and civilized. In lucid moments he discourses to Marlow with a voice that rings 'deep to the very last' (p. 147). The inner strife of intellect and appetite never ceases. To the end he maintains a fidelity to those same ideas he has mocked and corrupted in the wild. Only on the final night of his life does Kurtz also achieve a detachment similar to Marlow's. For a single instant he escapes, *as Marlow interprets it*, beyond blind egoism to the distance from which to judge and sum up.

> He cried in a whisper at some image, at some vision – he cried out twice, a cry that was no more than a breath –
> 'The horror! The horror!'
>
> (p. 149)

Kurtz's words are addressed perhaps to himself, perhaps to the void. They are a statement of reckoning, not a message. Whatever the specific vision he cries out at must remain still another enigma. What matters to Marlow, however, is not the particular object which brought forth the judgment but the act of judgment itself. The spoken word thus becomes a gesture towards meaning. It translates Kurtz's ultimate self-knowledge, which is the most 'you can hope' from life (p. 150), into the physical cry. And so Marlow transforms Kurtz once again and finally into a hero, and ratifies his act, indeed participates in it by interpreting this apparent impulse of judgment.

> After all, this was the expression of some sort of belief; it had candour, it had conviction, it had a vibrating note of revolt in its whisper, it had the appalling face of a glimpsed truth – the strange commingling of desire and hate. ... I like to think my summing up would not have been a word of careless contempt. Better his cry – much better. It was an affirmation, a moral victory paid for by innumerable defeats, by abominable terrors, by abominable satisfactions. But it was a victory!   (p. 151)

Having survived his own fever, the physical correlative to the spiritual struggle in the darkness with Kurtz, Marlow returns to Europe where two significant events yet remain: his visit to Kurtz's Intended and the telling of the tale aboard the *Nellie*. In the dusk of the sepulchral city, the Intended's light is the light of faith in Kurtz and of her fidelity to his memory. Yet her Kurtz is as much a fiction, has as little relation to the man buried in the Congo, as was Marlow's when he first declared his moral allegiance.

The reader, having travelled this far, knowing what Marlow knows, recognizes the simple dramatic irony and shares his discomfort when the Intended claims that Kurtz's 'goodness shone in every act' (p. 160). Marlow believes he owes Kurtz the truth; how much does he owe the woman's fragile fantasy? Once more the choice is between nightmares. She insists that Marlow join in her faith by reporting Kurtz's last words – which she believes she has guessed already. Wrung by the clash of the truth he possesses and the phantoms she cherishes, Marlow lies out of compassion, claiming that 'the last words he pronounced was – your name' (p. 161).

The web of fictions, of character and culture, still protects this woman from the wildernesses of soul and cosmos. Yet to rend the web with nothing to weave in its place would be a senseless cruelty. Marlow lies so that the Intended's beautiful, unreal, civilized world will not crash to the ground. The choice is one of human compassion, but *not* an affirmation of the falsehoods he leaves intact. He hardly feels the deed has been heroic, expecting that 'the house [will] collapse before [he can] escape, that the heavens [will] fall upon [his] head' (p. 162).

Marlow leaves unmolested society's myths for the Intended. But for the men who listen he recounts as best he can the truth of his experiences in the heart of darkness. Though they have shared the life of the sea in the past, as Director of Companies, Accountant, and Lawyer, they each now play a social role ashore. Marlow seeks to awaken them, as he was awakened, as Kurtz was finally awakened, to the illusions that support those roles, to a universe whose absolute contingency undermines complacent social identity, and to the dark energies within their souls which roles, characters, and civilization all conceal.

As he created Kurtz, so Marlow now creates himself as narrator—he too comes to have a social role aboard the *Nellie*. The determination he earlier displayed while coaxing the steamboat up the river makes him steadfast in his task of telling the tale, despite the galling awareness of how language fails him. The function of his social character, moreover, redefines the community; once the tale is finished the men on board share a fellowship which is neither their old bond of the sea nor the parts they play ashore. They sit in silence and darkness until their host, the Director, speaks with a verdict suggesting more than the immediate situation of the *Nellie*. And the primary narrator more fully reveals the change arising from an education paralleling Marlow's own. The vista before them has been transformed, penetrated with an equilibrium of tranquility and encroaching darkness.

'We have lost the first of the ebb,' said the Director, suddenly. I raised my head. The offing was barred by a black bank of clouds, and the tranquil waterway leading to the uttermost ends of the earth flowed sombre under an overcast sky – seemed to lead into the heart of an immense darkness. (p. 164)

That a story, despite all shortcomings, paleness, and failures of expression, can accomplish something of a moral education for those able to understand, underscores the potency of Marlow's heroism.

Having survived the romantic hero's momentum towards self-destruction, Marlow has assumed Kurtz's role. He has discovered, however, that the romantic hero has no place in a society that can no longer provide absolute structures of meaning and restraint to define himself against: a modern world in which the historical and ahistorical, the meaningful and the contingent, collide. Kurtz sought to subsume all dichotomies within his ego, and was torn apart instead. Only at the last could he detach himself and judge. Marlow, then, does not simply assume Kurtz's role as hero; he transforms it. He yokes together or comprehends those antinomies that destroyed Kurtz, not by the force of his will, but through his ironic perspective.

The general irony that thus comprehends enduring paradox represents a moral vision Marlow has earned in the course of the tale, much as Wilhelm Meister, Rastignac, and Pip achieve moral educations and social identities. Each creates for himself a new character and with it a role and responsibility in the world. Unlike the others, however, *Marlow is also responsible for creating the community that defines his character.*

A general irony that juxtaposes a radical scepticism and an enduring faith in a basic code of human behaviour, therefore, is not only the foundation of Marlow's character; it is a moral framework for new solidarity. (In *Lord Jim*, we shall see, it also structures the narrative itself.) As I have just argued, the primary narrator has been changed by Marlow's testimony to the degree that he now sees and describes the external world in imagery that echoes Marlow's. The fullest evidence of the meaningfulness of this unnamed narrator's own experience, surely, is that he too has felt compelled to recount the tale.

The art of Marlow's narrative is finally heroic only insofar as it is thus active in the world, establishing a direct relation between life and art through the understanding of the men who listen, and through the fellowship that grows from understanding. Yet the suspicion torments Marlow (and Conrad) that the contact between life and art is at best tenuous, at worst a chimera. The endeavour is heroic, but always suspect – always we sense Conrad's fear that to talk about life is a poor substitute for the full, immediate capacity to live and act. Conrad fully anticipates the more recent vogue among post-modern, post-structuralist critics who explore the unavoidable ironies at the heart of language and which undercut the validity of all symbolic expression.

The newly born fellowship on the *Nellie*, though it may be of short duration amidst the silence and darkness, is many a league from both the unconscious fidelity of the vanishing code of the sea – as aboard the *Narcissus* – and the pious egoism and moral self-delusions of the larger society ashore. Marlow has insisted that each of his listeners participate in the acts of interpretation and judgment. Each joins in achieving the story, as we readers must do through the mediation of the primary narrator. Ideally, to the extent we successfully realize the story, we too are educated and share in the fellowship. Yet the community of Marlow's audience is not one of unconscious identity – the truths from the heart of darkness must be individual to each member. Unavoidably, therefore, the same self-consciousness and ironic awareness that bind us together, also isolate us. Just as Marlow could recognize the impulse behind Kurtz's cry 'The horror!' while not fathoming its enigmatic, private meaning, he is haunted knowing he can never fully, or to his mind adequately, convey the reality of his experiences. Sceptical, with yet enough faith to persevere, he remains at the helm – he tells the tale.

2

Heroism and Narrative Form in *Lord Jim*

He existed for me, and after all it is only through me that he exists for you. I've led him out by the hand; I have paraded him before you.[1]

Lord Jim, begun before *Heart of Darkness* and finished afterwards, in 1900, more daringly evolves its narrative structure on the pattern of Marlow's ironic sensibility. The bold temporal displacement of events, the juxtaposition of widely divergent yet thematically related characters, the portrait of Jim spied through 'rents in a fog', all are responses to the collapse dramatised within *Lord Jim* of the moral foundations of the nineteenth-century realistic novel and, indeed, of Marlow's character. For Jim, heinously guilty and nonetheless 'one of us', tears Marlow from the cradle of self-satisfied complacency, and into a realm of half-light and moral uncertainty.

Marlow's education, though begun with his first glimpse of Jim, continues as he tells the tale at various times and for different audiences – the French lieutenant, Stein, as well as the 'privileged man' who receives the last of it. Their own new perspectives are accrued and added to the body of the tale in due order. The narrative's form thus generates meaning not simply by the climax and denouement of a traditional plot but by the relation of characters and events, including the various repetitions of the story itself, outside of historically defined sequence.[2] The method reflects Marlow's new vision: it comprehends alternative possibilities without forcing arbitrary resolution. Yet at the same time it imposes narrative form on a tale that ultimately denies all conventional boundary. As hero, then, and as artist, Marlow's task in *Lord Jim* is as ancient as it is modern; he strives to establish human meaning in the face of encroaching moral chaos. More immediately, he fulfils the responsibility he assumed early on for Jim with a portrait capturing without diminishing the contradictions of his character.

The opening paragraph, recounted by an unknown narrator, paints the most concrete portrait of Jim we ever receive. This is one instance of the initial narrator's marked self-assurance. For omniscient, deft, he never doubts his ability to represent simple, undissembling reality.

> He was an inch, perhaps two, under six feet, powerfully built, and he advanced straight at you with a slight stoop of the shoulders, head forward, and a fixed from-under stare which made you think of a charging bull. His voice was deep, loud, and his manner displayed a kind of dogged self-assertion which had nothing aggressive in it. It seemed a necessity, and it was directed apparently as much at himself as at anybody else. He was spotlessly neat, apparelled in immaculate white from shoes to hat, and in the various Eastern ports where he got his living as ship-chandler's water-clerk he was very popular.   (p. 3)

Marlow, by contrast, all too aware of contradiction and shadow, will never quite *see* Jim, at least not as a unified character, no matter the light or proximity.

Although the novel begins *in media res*, Jim serving as a water-clerk during those purgatorial years between his leap from the *Patna* and the glorious dream of Patusan, the initial narrator goes on to sketch Jim's life from childhood to *Patna* in a roughly linear pattern, with none of the temporal leaps, digressions, or juxtapositions characteristic of Marlow's later narration. A certainty of *story* prevails, of characters and events in meaningful, straightforward relation. By tracing the course of Jim's background, these early chapters establish the context of his failure. And the security of the narrator's perspective may be seen as sharing the same moral foundation as Jim.

> Originally he came from a parsonage. Many commanders of fine merchant-ships come from these abodes of piety and peace. Jim's father possessed such certain knowledge of the Unknowable as made for the righteousness of people in cottages without disturbing the ease of mind of those who an unerring Providence enables to live in mansions.   (p. 5)

Despite the mild social irony, we glimpse here a world in which, Mr Bennett in his study, Mr Pocket giving his lessons, the moral certainty of the social environment provides shared ideals for author, narrator, and audience. Pip can tell his story – we understand who he *is* – because he has synthesized his private self with socio-historical realities, has accepted his place and responsibilities within the social world, and thus, has achieved full character in the tradition of the nineteenth-century realistic novel.[3] Jim's heritage, common and well known, equally engenders expectations of how he will fulfil his part in the drama.

The shared moral ideals within this tradition also provide a secure foundation for narration and for judgment. When the initial narrator adopts a tone of casual irony, for example, the covert, 'true' meaning to be reconstructed by the reader is nearly as concrete as if it were manifest; for the assumption must be that narrator and reader understand each other, share moral standards, are of the right sort. We have little trouble in recognizing a betrayal of the straight line when Jim adopts 'another sentiment':

> To Jim that gossiping crowd, viewed as seamen, seemed at first more unsubstantial than so many shadows. But at length he found a fascination in the sight of those men, in their appearance of doing so well on such a small allowance of danger and toil. In time, beside the original disdain there grew up slowly another sentiment; and suddenly, giving up the idea of going home, he took a berth as chief mate of the *Patna*.   (p. 13)

Although Jim hails from the same parochial environment that nurtured moral realism, spiritually he has raised himself on the pap of 'light holiday literature' (p. 5). He has no desire to become, as Pip eventually does, a morally conscious one among many, but a hero whom the many will honour. This dream does not lead him to deny forthrightly the social code his father upholds; yet his romantic egoism sets the code at a distance; it is not a secure foundation for his identity. The narrative, having established the potential conflict between Jim's egoism and his duty, moves swiftly to the moment of crisis.

> The sharp hull driving on its way seemed to rise a few inches in succession through its whole length, as though it had become pliable, and settled down again rigidly to its work of cleaving the

smooth surface of the sea. Its quivering stopped, and the faint noise of thunder ceased all at once, as though the ship had steamed across a narrow belt of vibrating water and of humming air.   (p. 26)

Suddenly we are launched forward to find Jim in the witness-box. Only by hints and suggestions over the next hundred pages do the facts of the desertion of the *Patna* grow certain, well after Marlow has taken up the tale. The earlier omniscient narrator brings us to the threshold of the event and then disappears, for what follows lies beyond the conventions that have defined his role. We might well expect, in that earlier tradition, the tracing of the fallen man's moral education, as in *The Rise and Fall of Silas Lapham*. In *Lord Jim*, however, Jim's character remains strikingly impervious to change. It is Marlow who awakens to social truths he has never before dared question. Or yet again we might anticipate, as another conventional possibility, the playing-out of Jim's spiritual degeneration. This, in fact, is not far distant from Conrad's original scheme for the story, the heart of which would be completed with Jim's repugnant deed.[4] However, all of Marlow's early involvement with Jim is aimed at forestalling precisely that sort of decline.

It struck me that it is from such as he that the great army of waifs and strays is recruited, the army that marches down, down into all the gutters of the earth. As soon as he left my room, that 'bit of shelter,' he would take his place in the ranks, and begin the journey towards the bottomless pit.   (p. 262)

From the moment Marlow senses that no single perspective or traditional standard will suffice for judgment, and strives to fathom Jim as something more than a pariah, *Lord Jim* evolves beyond the paradigm of moral realism as surely as Jim is cast out from the ranks of the faithful.

To a far greater degree than in *Heart of Darkness*, Marlow has himself been a committed member of the conservative profession of the sea. No solitary wanderer of the globe, he captains a commercial ship; his identity is tied to the larger solidarity of the craft. Nor is he innocent. He prides himself on his lack of illusion. As in 'Youth', his romantic dreams have long ago been dispelled. His acceptance of his role and fate, unlike Jim's, lies 'in the perfect love of the work' (p. 10). This vision of experience, of having seen the world for what he believes it to be, is tinged with complacency. If Marlow has accepted that he will never attain the glory of Captain Brierly, that he is ageing and disillusioned, his character is nevertheless so thoroughly anchored to hallowed consolations of the sea that he gains deep satisfaction – reassurance of his own identity and meaningfulness – by training boys to follow in their turn.

> The sea has been good to me, but when I remember all these boys that passed through my hands, some grown up now and some drowned by this time, but all good stuff for the sea, I don't think I have done badly by it either.   (pp. 44–5)

Jim too, of course, appears superficially of the same breed when Marlow spots him, standing 'there for all the parentage of his kind' (p. 43), with the other disgraced officers of the *Patna*. Marlow's initial impulse is to judge him as a captain must judge one who has broken faith.

> I waited to see him overwhelmed, confounded, pierced through and through, squirming like an impaled beetle – and I was half afraid to see it too – if you can understand what I mean. Nothing more awful than to watch a man who has been found out, not in a crime but in a more than criminal weakness. (p. 42)

Yet what drives Marlow nearly to rage and, ironically, later to assume responsibility for Jim, is the disturbing paradox apparent from the first; the man-boy is caught between the other scoundrels, whose guilt he shares, and the community he has betrayed.

Jim's leap from the *Patna* represents a darker side of the cycle of innocence and experience in 'Youth'. In the earlier story a complementary balance exists between the romantic illusions of the young Marlow and his worldly wisdom thirty years later. The older man gains consolation through renewed contact with his youth; he will wither, but the seaman's traditions endure. As I argued in Chapter 1, the structural irony of the primary narrator enhances rather than undercuts the sustaining equilibrium between innocence and experience, and represents Conrad's abiding belief that a seaman's life earns a meaning, an immortality of sorts, through his participation in the ancient and ageless struggle with the sea.

Jim, however, shatters cycle and consolation. He might easily have been any one of the boys Captain Marlow has nurtured to a role in the great sustaining pageant of the sea. The deed of Jim's social betrayal strips from Marlow the comfortable, reinforcing assumptions on which his character has rested, much as did, by stages, the journey up the Congo in *Heart of Darkness*. There Marlow created a Kurtz, a fiction woven of legend, hearsay, hopes, only for it to collide with the fact of the real Kurtz's savagery. In *Lord Jim* the undeniable fact of social betrayal appears early on; Marlow's relationship with Jim is a response to the implications of that fact. Over a period of years he attempts to find an excuse for what happened or at least the satisfaction of fuller understanding. The result is a portrait of Jim's character similar in form to the early, imaginary Kurtz: a patchwork of perspectives, reports, paradoxes, and illuminations, existing outside of the linear historical dimensions of the tale.

An essential element of this portrait is the testimony, judgments, and reactions of other characters, especially those who in some sense are recognized as conventional heroes. Marlow must be seen as both one of those witnesses and, finally, as narrator and hero in his own right – a modern hero – someone who transcends their limited understanding.

If such a one as Jim can succumb, when caught unawares, to a deep weakness within himself – perhaps so simple a weakness as a desire to live when balked by fate at every turn – then anyone may be vulnerable. Surely this is the sense of the great Brierly's leap into the sea. Brierly has never been tested, or so he fears, as Jim has been. Due to luck or unmatched skill, he has never had to come to terms with his own mortal limitations or the possibility of failure, as perforce Marlow and other more ordinary mortals have had to do. It may be that one *must* make this compromise with oneself, accepting consolation rather than unqualified glory, before the internal ethical foundation of maturity and social character can be formed. Brierly remains an innocent; his self-esteem is 'grounded on ... external and insecure foundations'.[5] Like Kurtz, Brierly is hollow at the core. Not the restraints of his own character but the external structure of his role has disguised secret impulses or weaknesses that he never before suspected. Jim's example reveals Brierly to himself; he discovers both the impermissible instincts and the fact that he lacks the fortitude to restrain them. Unable to bear the thought that someday his own secret weakness may be found out, he seeks to leave his reputation intact, if clouded with mystery.

The human weakness revealed in Jim's behaviour which undoes
Brierly is neither a surprise nor greatly troubling to the French
lieutenant. Where Brierly's heroism concealed an inner hollowness,
the lieutenant to all appearance is leaden and undistinguished, save
for a pair of scars earned as duty demanded. Although he remained
on the crippled *Patna* for thirty hours, he is no stranger to fear and
self-doubt:

> 'Each of them – I say each of them, if he were an honest man –
> *bien entendu* – would confess that there is a point – somewhere a
> point when you let go everything (*vous lachez tout*). And you have
> got to live with that truth – do you see? Given a certain
> combination of circumstances, fear is sure to come. ... And even
> for those who do not believe this truth there is fear all the same –
> the fear of themselves.'   (p. 146)

With the bearing of a village priest, the lieutenant is an oracle for
the solidarity of the community. Paul Bruss argues persuasively,
however, that as smug, pompous, and narrow-minded as the
French lieutenant is, to see him as an avatar of self-sacrificing
heroism is to under-value Marlow's irony.[6] Surely we should be
wary of the lieutenant's testimony – he, like Brierly and like Stein to
come, is flawed. Nevertheless, the simple fact of his faithfulness to
duty when sent aboard the *Patna* is undeniable, and much of
Marlow's pique may be attributed to his awareness that this stolid
priest of social weal has earned the right to his say. To him, as to the
initial narrator, the facts are clear and unmistakable, and all of
Marlow's sympathetic perceptions of Jim's predicament seem
irrelevant. Not a little irony may be seen in the encounter, for
Marlow is half-heartedly contesting those same absolute standards
of fidelity that have sustained his own mature identity.

Marlow's narrative juxtaposes the perspectives of Brierly and the
French lieutenant, not according to temporal congruity – his
meetings with the two are years apart – but thematically. Brierly and
the lieutenant are two of several characters in *Lord Jim* who are
recognized as heroes either by Marlow, by their peers, or by society
at large. Although markedly flawed, each represents a standard or
touchstone by which to judge Jim's failure on the *Patna* and his
deeds in Patusan. Marlow too, if we are to see that he is moving
towards a new form of heroism, must be brought into relation to
these others. While each of them is limited by a particular, narrow

perspective, which also determines his heroic behaviour, Marlow alone seeks to achieve a broader vision.

Marlow admits that his own early involvement with Jim arose from the hope of discovering an excuse that would, by laying the immediate case to rest, leave the moral order of his own life unchallenged.

> I see well enough now that I hoped for the impossible – for the laying of what is the most obstinate ghost of man's creation, of the uneasy doubt uprising like a mist, secret and gnawing like a worm, and more chilling than the certitude of death – the doubt of the sovereign power enthroned in a fixed standard of conduct.
>
> (p. 50)

The day-to-day details of Marlow's career do apparently remain unchanged. Yet the moral fabric which underpinned daily responsibilities as well as larger issues of identity and purpose has been ripped free. The codes binding individual to community appear illusory if not capricious. The social world's ability to fend off external chaos through habit and duty is thus imperilled. Crumbling as well are the foundations of moral realism, of the initial narrator's clear-sighted certainty, of the possibilities of art. The task Marlow undertakes in staying true to Jim and in telling the tale is no less than to reweave the moral fabric of human endeavour.

II

Another artist competes with Marlow throughout *Lord Jim*; Jim intends himself as the raw stuff for heroic lore which he sketches many times in his imagination before committing his hand to the creation of Patusan. And his heroism, like his art, complements Marlow's; neither is complete without the other. For each man, furthermore, the success of his art determines that of his heroism.

From childhood, Jim's imagination has painted a world in counterpoint to his father's parsonage, to his first training ship, and to the sea-going ships on which he has been an officer. When besieged by the unromantic claims of his daily round, he has 'live[d] in his mind the sea-life of light literature' (p. 6). This egoistic imagination is fundamentally anti-social, cutting Jim off from his fellows as well as from the immediate life about him. He

creates himself – or rather, an ideal vision of himself – over and over
again as the hero of simple plots plagiarized from pulp fiction. While
Marlow's art strives like the traditional frame narrative to create a
bridge between the community and the scorned and scorning
solitary, Jim bothers with no such complexity. The others in his
imaginary romances exist solely to ratify and celebrate him, while
the communities of his ships must let him earn his bread and dream
until the opportunity for heroism appears.

Such chances do, in fact, arise. Aboard the training ship he could
take his place in the cutter during a gale and fly to the aid of a
shipwreck; he could remain at his post on the *Patna* until the French
steamer's arrival. Each act would have earned him a measure of
glory, though shared with others or muted by being no more than
what duty demanded. Yet at each crisis he fails. And it is his
imagination, the very source of his heroic image, that undoes him. It
projects numbing horrors on to reality – of a malevolent universe
directing its fury especially at him, of hundreds of pilgrims dying in
agony with him as their impotent witness.

> He stood still looking at these recumbent bodies, a doomed man
> aware of his fate, surveying the silent company of the dead. They
> *were* dead! Nothing could save them! There were boats enough for
> half of them perhaps, but there was no time. No time! No time! It
> did not seem worth while to open his lips, to stir hand or foot.
> Before he could shout three words, or make three steps, he would
> be floundering in a sea whitened awfully by the desperate
> struggles of human beings, clamorous with the distress of cries
> for help.   (p. 86)

Conjured in his mind, these scenes gather a momentum of their
own, becoming more tangible than the readily apparent dangers.

Like the egoism of Donkin and Wait in *The Nigger of the 'Narcissus'*
and of Kurtz in *Heart of Darkness*, an egoistic imagination makes Jim
unworthy of the trust that a community must place in its members. It becomes the 'soft spot' through which the normal functions
of social character and culture collapse – these fail to protect Jim
from being overwhelmed by his own fears, for they no longer define
his identity. No strength, no refuge lies in duty if one's sense of self-
worth has a far different source. In the welter of crisis, consciousness
and the unconscious, courage and fear, dream and reality clash.
Imagination, which has impelled him towards a new self-generated

character, alienates him irrevocably from the old. His failure of duty aboard the *Patna* cuts Jim off from the 'parentage of his kind'.

This pattern of imagination isolating individual from community is a common element of romanticism – one need think only of Werther, Waverley, or Manfred. Yet for Jim – until he arrives in Patusan – imagination cripples his ability to act, rather than providing courage beyond the reach of the average man, and seals him off from the natural world, rather than opening his senses to it. He is torn between the demands of a romantic imperative of uncompromising courage, to which he aspires, and the fears born of a self-conscious egoism. So heightened is his sense of horrific consequences that he lacks that impulsive first step of a Bob Stanton, going down with his ship because a terrified lady's-maid refuses to flee for safety, or of a Stein, slumping in his saddle as if dead, coolly awaiting the approach of his attackers. Marlow shares sympathetically something of Jim's weakness and his guilt. More than this, he comes to sense a deep kinship in the discovery that to create a world, a story – which both he and Jim are about – may be at the expense of living fully within the world. For despite his odd disclaimer that he has 'no imagination' (p. 223), by the end of the tale, Jim dead and Patusan dismembered, each surviving only through the narrative, Marlow himself has become incorporeal, no longer even a voice in the darkness, but withdrawn to written testimony for a solitary audience. Little sense remains of the robustly successful captain of commercial ships. The gesture is faint, private, and, nevertheless, heroic.

One character in *Lord Jim* who most certainly has lived in the world is Stein. Thoroughly a romantic – the same verdict he pronounces on Jim – Stein has led not one but a series of successful careers. As Marlow recounts the story of the *Patna* and of Jim's successive attempts as a water-clerk, Stein also senses kindred instincts, though not quite the same that Marlow feels. Indeed, Jim may be seen as a transitional figure caught between two possibilities of heroism: Stein's, a romantic model who belongs already to a vanishing era, and Marlow's, whose distinctively modern heroism is bred largely out of the lesson of Jim's own disaster.

Stein and Jim are both romantic in this one fundamental sense; they have imagined ideal visions of what they wish to be. Stein, however, like Singleton, belongs to a nobler, passing generation. His romantic idealism was weaned on the revolutionary movement of 1848 – which Conrad, the exiled Pole and son of revolutionaries, would especially honour – and he has never ceased pursuing the dream he has fashioned. As it has changed, so has he, as Marlow testifies:

> I saw only the reality of his destiny, which he had known how to follow with unfaltering footsteps, that life begun in humble surroundings, rich in generous enthusiasms, in friendship, love, war – in all the exalted elements of romance.   (p. 217)

Jim's idealized vision of himself has a far different source – the light adventure novels of his childhood. Unlike Stein, Jim is never eager or able on his own to wed his dreams to the reality of this world. Marlow condemns in Jim as his 'sublimated, idealized selfishness' (p. 177), what he praises in Stein. Jim has awaited amidst his dreams for the intervening hand of providence; Stein has explored, married, found a war–comrade, established a company whose reach throughout the archipelago has the vitality of a living creature. To change the world as well as oneself according to a noble dream, as Stein has done repeatedly, is not so selfish, Marlow suggests, as Jim's smug passivity.

III

With Stein's ring and Marlow's (empty) revolver in hand, Jim arrives in Patusan to create Patusan. Another leap, this one from Rajah Allang's stockade, then still another into a mud bank from which he claws his way, bring him into the Bugis settlement. Covered with primal ooze, unable to hold himself upright, he is carried into Doramin's presence, the raw stuff of a man, unborn, half-dead, yet on the threshold of form and life. Both come to him, along with the undeniable validation as hero, during his dream-like and unabashedly romantic adventures. We should remember, however, that the legend survives in Marlow's testimony, a tale that embraces the unresolvable paradoxes of Jim's history and character. As Jim creates temporary order on the formlessness of Patusan, Marlow is a hero whose art imposes form on a story whose deep truths seem to deny all form and meaning.

The disparate elements of Patusan are as raw as Jim standing before Doramin. Intrigue and fear have made life uncertain amidst the chaos. Jim seizes this political turmoil to shape with his hand. His new character and the new political realities of Patusan emerge in a symbiotic relation.

Jim brings order to Patusan in the romantic, straightforward terms of his imagination. The village's history from the day of his arrival until Marlow's visit is a drama for which Jim is both playwright and hero. This effort to fashion social order along the lines of a romantic script parallels Marlow's later struggle to project form on the tale. Yet Jim's sense of story is more closely akin to that of the novel's initial narrator. He never questions his perspective; events are meaningful, speak for themselves – as he has arranged them. The persuasion of the Bugis, the already legendary storming of Sherif Ali's camp, the cowed terror of Rajah Allang, are all deftly orchestrated elements of the tale Jim has foreseen almost from the first. He recounts the story to Marlow, proud and bashful and exuberant. Others already have it wrong; legends evolve apparently by the hour. Jim knows the *truth* of the matter, and never doubts.

> Jim [would] stamp his foot in vexation and exclaim with an exasperated little laugh, 'What can you do with such silly beggars? They will sit up half the night talking bally rot, and the greater the lie the more they seem to like it.'   (p. 266)

The self-assurance with which Jim deals with daily exigencies is in keeping with his faith in the narrative order he perceives in events. These, in turn, render to him clear, unalloyed meanings. He possesses an absolute faith in discoverable truth behind superficial confusion. Never do the limitations of his perspective, let alone conflicting tales or competing evidence, deter him from performing the role of Solomon. Although Jim's dilemma during the inquiry revealed to Marlow how misleading even the clearest of facts can be, Jim himself seems untouched by the experience. No mystery in Patusan lies beyond his fathoming. To Marlow he tells the story of an old man whose wife has dishonoured him by giving away three brass pots. Jim sets off through the forest as sovereign adjudicator, put out at the bother but never doubting his ability finally to set the problem right.

> Got him the infernal pots back of course – and pacified all hands. No trouble to settle it. Of course not. Could settle the deadliest quarrel in the country by crooking his little finger.   (p. 269)

By establishing social harmony, Jim succeeds, as Stein had, where Kurtz failed. He imports such alien Western ideals as free trade for the poorest natives as well as, certainly, for the economic benefit of Stein's trading company. The point is part and parcel of an entire system of 'noble ideas' Jim intends for the enlightenment of the wilderness. Ironically enough, these ideals belong to the same code of human behaviour that Jim betrayed on the *Patna*. He alone, however, is unaware of how arbitrary his new law is – that given his power and influence any decree, no matter its nature, would bear the same weight.

> Jim began to speak. Resolutely, coolly, and for some time he enlarged upon the text that no man should be prevented from getting his food and his children's food honestly. [Rajah Allang] sat like a tailor at his board, one palm on each knee, his head low, and fixing Jim through the grey hair that fell over his very eyes. When Jim had done there was a great stillness. Nobody seemed to breathe even; no one made a sound till the old Rajah sighed faintly, and looking up, with a toss of his head said quickly, 'You hear, my people! No more of these little games.'
>
> (p. 250)

Arbitrary or not, most of the community welcome stability. None doubts that political peace depends on Jim. Patusan needs him in order to survive in its new organization. Equally, Jim needs the unqualified praise of Patusan to validate his new character as hero. For in the eyes of these villagers he is free of the secret sin that he can never forget. Like Brierly, Jim's self-image has come to be harnessed to the regard of others, to the constant reinforcement of his value and valour in the eyes of the world – even the little world of Patusan.

Yet as is typical of the romantic hero, Jim's identity is not generated within or bounded by the community. The people of Patusan trust him to decide the issues of their lives, large and small, political peace and family squabbles – one recalls Moses besieged by the Israelites in the wilderness with demands for justice. And Jim's inner peace is sanctified by that great trust. Yet though the two, Jim and Patusan, depend on each other, their identities never merge; he never enters the fold. Creator and guarantor of Patusan, Jim remains, one foot in the settlement, the other in the wilderness of his solitude.

Because the town depends so thoroughly upon him, while he continues so intractably distinct from it, this work of art, this romantic Patusan, remains too much a creature of Jim's imagination; it fails finally to coalesce as an independent community. It has no secure life of its own. The Bugis and the peasants are pleased with Jim's handiwork; Rajah Allang and his followers submit out of fear. All recognize that it cannot be sustained without Jim. They are players in his drama; their wills, desires and fears subordinated to the authority of his dream.

Knowing that in the past white men have stayed but a while, sensing that Jim's spirit remains detached from their own, Doramin seeks to extend the political responsibility, lobbying with Marlow during his visit for Dain Waris to be made titular ruler. Doramin's ambitions for his son are scarcely concealed. Nevertheless, by producing leaders from within, the political structure might generate validity and independent life. That same process is dramatized by Conrad in *Nostromo* as Sulaco evolves from the precarious private dreams of a few into the momentum of shared history. Yet although Dain Waris is his closest friend, spiritual brother, and advisor, Jim apparently never addresses the possibility of surrendering his private dream to the community's independence – to do so would risk surrendering himself.

When Marlow visits Patusan he recognizes that the new social order Jim has created remains largely an illusion. In a further irony, therefore, Jim's very success again undermines Marlow's faith in an absolute standard of conduct. For clearly in Patusan such a standard has no security beyond Jim's ability to enforce it. Jim's single-handed, single-minded projection of liberal values only highlights the general truth of man's battle with chaos. His heroism exposes, at least in Marlow's eyes, the frailty of the values that are its foundation. Marlow will bring many of the same values – now relative rather than absolute – into juxtaposition with a radical scepticism as the foundation for his own heroic endeavour.

During his visit, however, he possesses already enough of an ironic awareness to sense not only that the code of the new community is arbitrary, but that the dream – and its dreamer/artist – abide within the frame of a threatening darkness. Marlow's intimation arises from no single suggestion during his journey to Patusan, but belongs to the new understanding thrust on him from the time of the *Patna* inquiry. Because all of Jim's successes are qualified for Marlow by his privileged knowledge of the former trespass – as they are for Jim himself – the serenity of Patusan seems a fragile illusion threatened by all of a besieging reality. Even as Jim is in the midst of reciting the tale of storming Sherif Ali's encampment, Marlow gazes off across village and wilderness towards the sea, the landscape's impression reflecting, as so often in Conrad, his own inner turmoil:

> I sat on the stump of a tree at his feet, and below us stretched the land, the great expanse of the forests, sombre under the sunshine, rolling like a sea, with glints of winding rivers, the grey spots of villages, and here and there a clearing, like an islet of light amongst the dark waves of continuous tree-tops. A brooding gloom lay over this vast and monotonous landscape; the light fell on it as if into an abyss. (p. 264)

We should recognize, nevertheless, that the sense of surrounding shadow also throws Jim's real achievement into starker relief. For a little while he has set his fate at a distance, if not ultimately mastered it. As romantic artist and hero he has at last formed a union between the ideals of his imagination and the physical world. The story of Stein's life with his 'poor Mohammed Bonso', his wife and daughter, is a similar brief sojourn of happiness, ended as with the blowing out of a match.

This pattern of tiny Camelots embattled by encroaching dangers recurs throughout Conrad's canon. The *Narcissus* struggling through nature's gales and human dissension, Marlow creating in the night a new fellowship aboard the *Nellie*, Sulaco facing threats from without and self-deception and treacheries within, Heyst's short-lived happiness, all embody the conflict between human hopes and an ever-threatening universe. This enduring dichotomy reflects the vision of irony Marlow achieves during the central action of *Lord Jim* and then, as narrator, uses to structure the tale. His sense of general irony, which I have discussed at length in Chapter 1, is indeed a moral vision, a response to the norms and values of the realism represented in *Lord Jim* by the initial narrator from whom Marlow assumes responsibility for the tale. The 'fixed standard of conduct' is no longer adequate; it is replaced with the ironic juxtaposition of such fundamental human values as solidarity, labour, and love, against a radical scepticism.

The uneasy equilibrium of faith and scepticism also mirrors the unresolvable paradox of Jim's nature – that he is 'one of us', a hero and artist, while equally cut off by his egoism, criminally culpable, a fraud. Gentleman Brown plays his deadly game by manipulating in his conversation with Jim a similar duality between honour and treachery, innocence and guilt. He engages Jim's imagination, instinctively painting a picture of common trials between them and demanding fair treatment according to the code of honour Jim has betrayed on the *Patna* and wed to his dream in Patusan. Brown will savagely scorn that code to avenge himself. Jim's true guilt for the débâcle remains moot; what matters is his own belief that he is responsible, that success or failure must be 'on his head'.

That same price has hung over each of his great enterprises in Patusan, and now he insists on redeeming himself with payment. His final act, accepting death at the hands of Doramin, fulfils the paradox within his own character. In death Jim celebrates his intense egoism and romantic imagination by indulging in dramatic self-sacrifice, and satisfies the 'soft spot', the self-destructive yearning for sleep, escape, peace, which has cursed him throughout. The spectacle of these final moments is inescapably heroic – certainly Jim, with his 'proud and unflinching glance' (p. 416), believes the point made – and so Marlow avows. Yet if Jim has transcended one paradox, he opens another. For his heroism perverts Stein's commitment to life after his own tragedy. Jim flies to the last parade of romantic egoism, choosing the grand gesture to consummate his idealized selfishness in death, rather than live with Jewel in a world as flawed as his own soul.

IV

Marlow's heroism answers Jim's, as does his art. And this new, modern heroism *is* Marlow's art; he fulfils his responsibility to Jim and to his own moral identity by creating a narrative the form of which – its thematic or spatial juxtapositions – is an analogue to the relativism of general irony. Yet Marlow's is an ancient labour as well; he struggles to create meaning where all seems meaningless, to affirm human values where chaos scorns all value. The narrative breaks down the simple, linear pattern we might expect if Jim were telling his own tale, as well as the assumptions and self-assurance underlying that pattern. Jim's romantic sensibility, like the moral realism of the initial narrator, cannot deal with competing perspectives, equivocation, and paradox.

Certainly Marlow tells a story in which a series of related events unfolds; but his narrative scrambles the order of events and characters, establishing relation and contrast, so that the Jim he weaves may be apprehended outside of temporal constraints. Jim exists for the reader as an accretion of perspectives and judgments, of events and counter-balancing stories-within-stories.

Not least of the ironies of Jim and Marlow as competing artists is Marlow's refusal to let Jim define himself. As a romantic, Jim seeks to pattern himself on the single glorious standard of his idealized model. Marlow is in fact his audience; he must *understand*, Jim pleads, the truth of the *Patna* as well as of Patusan. Yet in Marlow's account various characters judge Jim based on their own predilections and weaknesses, while others report to Marlow events he has not witnessed. The history leading to Jim's death, for example, is passed on through Brown's death-bed ecstasy, Jewel's fury, and Tamb' Itam's stupefaction; Jim for once cannot speak for himself, and Marlow, as usual, is far removed from the scene. Each perspective with its set of biases possesses an element of truth. Gentleman Brown senses from the start a deep, perverse kinship with someone who has called himself a 'gentleman' yet has broken faith with the code that makes such a word meaningful. In his prescription for Jim, Stein has revealed a sympathy only for those impulses he shares. Even Cornelius, servile and despicable, repeatedly scores a telling point, that Jim is only a 'child'. Yet as with our earlier discussion of Brierly and the lieutenant, no single view possesses more than a limited validity.

As a character of the central tale, Marlow has his own limitations. He too is trapped by the emotions or circumscribed vantage of a given moment. Although he lacks the narrow biases of other characters, his attitude towards Jim vacillates from indignation to identification, from emotional weariness to repeated intercessions. As narrator, however, Marlow's broader, ironic perspective seeks to transcend the constraints of a particular historical moment. Of course, even this more detached perspective has the limitations of its context. Yet the central tale and the narrative frame are not discrete to the same extent as in *Heart of Darkness*. In *Lord Jim* they interpenetrate. Marlow recounts Jim's story to the French lieutenant; his response becomes an integral accretion to the yarn. Thus, Marlow continues to create Jim, gathering perspectives and telling the tale as means and method for understanding him. The resulting portrait of Jim also exists outside the simple dynamics of the plot or even the stable perspective of any single narrative vantage; it is fully realized only in the reader's active recognition of juxtapositions, harmonies, and paradoxes.

At the same time, the portrait reflects one of the most striking ways in which Jim stays true to himself: the static quality of his own character. Despite the multiplicity of perspectives, he remains essentially unchanged, as enigmatic as ever, at the moment of his death, clad in white and lost within the ideal vision of his imagination, as when he jumped off the *Patna*. Circumstances have changed, not he. A tone of voice, a confession, contradiction upon contradiction, the hero and the coward, dreamer and doer, Jim slowly grows in the reader's mind, not with coherence and clear outlines, but with the fragmented disorder-within-order of a Braque painting.

> The views he let me have of himself were like those glimpses through the shifting rents in a thick fog – bits of vivid and vanishing detail, giving no connected idea of the general aspect of a country. They fed one's curiosity without satisfying it; they were no good for purposes of orientation.   (p. 76)

Although Jim's character may be static, unchanging from beginning to end, no two readers, given the demands on their sympathies and powers of discrimination, will ever see him in the same light. For that matter, a reader's judgment of Jim will inevitably evolve from one encounter to the next, as Albert Guerard has pointed out in arguing that Jim is far more culpable than Marlow's strategy allows us to perceive at first glance.[7] Like Jim himself, however, Guerard searches for a single *correct* perspective; this misguided impulse seeks a resolution to the paradoxes which in fact lie at the novel's heart. Marlow's narrative, reflecting as it does his ironic vision, never allows the security of such firm ground.

This narrative irony plays two further vital roles in *Lord Jim*. It selects and orders the competing perspectives and digressions, which acquire meaning in relation to the whole only as the reader, in turn, actively recognizes their correlation. And, with its stubborn dualism of faith and scepticism, this sense of irony guides Marlow and the attentive reader beyond the limitations of any single perspective. With Marlow we tread our way through the judgments of Brierly, the lieutenant, Stein, Cornelius, and others. The truth of Jim's ineluctable character lies always in between and silent.

To the extent that Marlow's vision of general irony is reflected both within the central tale – the essential paradox he spies in Jim's character, for example – and in the narrative structure of thematic juxtaposition, the traditional distinction between form and content collapses. In another sense, however, form and content remain very much at odds. Another crucial aspect of Marlow's heroism lies in the way his art imposes narrative form on a tale that, in its complex antinomies, apparently denies all form and boundary. This is a modern version of the eternal heroic quest, seeking to subjugate the chaos of the universe to human artifice and meaning.

This particular struggle of Marlow's begins on a primary level. Language itself *is* form, of course, and man's most basic tool for ordering the universe around him. As Jewel describes the death of her mother, for example, Marlow is drawn once again from the shelter of self-imposed custom, as he had been earlier by Jim's betrayal of duty.

> For a moment I had a view of a world that seemed to wear a vast and dismal aspect of disorder. ... I seemed to have lost all my words in the chaos of dark thoughts I had contemplated for a second or two beyond the pale. These came back, too, very soon, for words also belong to the sheltering conception of light and order which is our refuge.   (p. 313)

As with so many other characters in *Lord Jim*, Jewel's perspective is terribly limited. Marlow 'knows' more than she, has a greater breadth of vision as well as of experience. And yet, the intensity of her doubts and suffering overwhelm him, carry him to another confrontation with primal confusion. Despite or because of his ironic detachment, he is impotent in dealing with immediate human sorrows and tragedy. In his words lies no solace for her. Nevertheless, in recalling the moment, as in the novel as a whole, Marlow later projects form upon formlessness, captures some sense of the ineffable, by describing the scene through language and story.

Like the other tensions within *Lord Jim*, the struggle towards form and meaning never ends. Twice Marlow 'finishes' the story, yet each conclusion denies full resolution. The first ending comes after Marlow has visited Jim in Patusan and witnessed his triumph. Even so, he remains uneasy. The unresolved tension heightens the reader's sense of Jim's achievement and of its fragility. Jim himself remains isolated, and all questions of fate and future are left open. Thus, Marlow's last glimpse of him:

> He was white from head to foot, and remained persistently visible with the stronghold of night at his back, the sea at his feet, the opportunity by his side – still veiled. ... For me that white figure in the stillness of coast and sea seemed to stand at the heart of a vast enigma. (p. 336)

Rather than sharing a new fellowship as aboard the *Nellie*, Marlow's audience in *Lord Jim* drifts away, 'as if the last image of that incomplete story, its incompleteness itself, and the very tone of the speaker, had made discussion vain and comment impossible' (p. 337). Although each man carries away 'like a secret' his private impression of the tale, the breaking up of Marlow's audience is another suggestion of the troubling vision in *Lord Jim*. No readily apparent community of understanding is generated here. The men listening drift away. So Marlow too. From no specific time or place, from out of the great silence itself appears his letter to the 'privileged man', the only one who 'showed an interest in [Jim] that survived the telling of his story'(p. 338).

The novel's final conclusion is no more complete, though its event – Jim's death – would resolve a traditional narrative suitably enough. While the shooting soon brings the story to a close, it fails to answer the central questions that have haunted Marlow from his first sight of Jim. The paradox of Jim's character, like the duality of Marlow's ironic sensibility, remains forever unresolved. This precludes the comfortable closure of a linear narrative developing through time towards climax and satisfying denouement. No grand summing up or final judgment, for which Marlow had so praised Kurtz, is here possible.

> And besides, the last word is not said, – probably shall never be said. Are not our lives too short for that full utterance which through all our stammerings is of course our only and abiding intention? I have given up expecting those last words, whose ring, if they could only be pronounced, would shake both heaven and earth. There is never time to say our last word – the last word of our love, of our desire, faith, remorse, submission, revolt.
> (p. 225)

Although his listeners may drift away, Marlow creates a picture, a story of Patusan that survives long after disaster has broken upon the village. Jim created a vital, living, doomed Patusan, held together by the energy of his will and, because of that, not a community capable of surviving in its own right. It thrives and then dies with all the intensity of Jim's imagination. Where Jim's Patusan is so full of life, Marlow's is static, more detached. Yet Marlow's Patusan endures; in the translation from memory to a story shared with others it lives as art lives. Patusan lives free of Marlow in a way it could never be free of Jim.

> I felt that when to-morrow I had left [Patusan] for ever, it would slip out of existence, to live only in my memory till I myself passed into oblivion. I have that feeling about me now; perhaps it is that feeling which has incited me to tell you the story, to try to hand over to you, as it were, its very existence, its reality – the truth disclosed in a moment of illusion. (p. 323)

As we have seen, of all Marlow's audience only one continues to express a concern for Jim's fate. What I have claimed to be Marlow's essentially modern heroism is qualified at every turn, as is most every other element of *Lord Jim*.

As the two Patusans are necessary to each other, so are the two men. Marlow is not simply Jim's friend, mentor, and father confessor; he provides a spiritual bridge to the society from which Jim has exiled himself, but to which he feels he must remain faithful. The ideal self-image Jim has pursued still defines itself according to standards of a world lost to him.

In turn, having accepted responsibility for Jim after the *Patna* incident, Marlow's continuing effort to understand him, to create a record of his character, to help him live, all constitute for the older man 'a struggle of moral survival'.[8] His responsibility and his identity have become intertwined; how Marlow fulfils his duty to Jim determines his success as artist, hero, and human being.

Marlow's vision of general irony, born of his endeavour to comprehend Jim, fulfils itself by shaping a tale whose form reflects that perception of enduring, unresolvable paradox in both the individual character and the nature of the world. And the tale, in turn, discharges at last Marlow's moral responsibility for him, producing a portrait which snatches him from the mutability of time and the tyranny of fate he carried within himself.

3

Watching the Orchards Robbed: Dowell and *The Good Soldier*

And if everything is so nebulous about a matter so elementary as the morals of sex, what is there to guide us in the more subtle morality of all other personal contacts, associations, and activities?[1]

John Dowell is an unlikely hero – the least likely, perhaps, of any of the narrators of this study. A cuckold of extraordinary blindness, by all indications a virgin though twelve years married, his personal history begins and ends with the role of nursemaid for women unwilling or unable to return his affection. A catalogue of critics decrying his supposed spiritual as well as physical impotence would be substantial; Mark Schorer, for example, claims that in *The Good Soldier* 'passionate situations are related by a narrator who is himself incapable of passion, sexual and moral alike'.[2] And John G. Hessler in a more recent article dismisses the possibility of Dowell's moral growth: 'His narrative does not represent any progress of the heart, any coming to insight.'[3] Yet albeit lame and isolated, Dowell is very much what my first sentence posits – a hero – both in the context of Ford Madox Ford's other novels and as a narrator who undergoes a moral education, tells his tale as a means of imposing order on chaos, and makes a final heroic gesture of human responsibility and love.

The structure of Dowell's frame narrative is neither static nor a completed circle as in *Heart of Darkness*, *The Great Gatsby*, and *The Sun Also Rises*. The narrators of those works possess relatively stable points of view in time and space. The experiences they recount are securely behind them. As in *Lord Jim*, however, the narration of *The Good Soldier* takes place over an extended period, while events of the

central tale continue to unfold, modifying perspectives on all that
has come before. The narrative *evolves*. Characters, events, and
judgments are revealed and juxtaposed, then sorted anew. This
form, this evolution, is a correlative to Dowell's own growth. His
transformation of Ashburnham from a slightly stupid hypocrite into
a romantic hero represents a new moral sensibility for Dowell
himself. And he chooses to be Nancy Rufford's protector, as he had
not chosen to be his wife's nursemaid. This, like his transformation
of Ashburnham, is an act of freedom and of love. By the end he has
discovered in himself a deep, formerly unsuspected, capacity for
love. He pairs it with a new radical scepticism – a perspective of
general irony, which again marks the fulfilment of a narrator's
education. The Marlow of *Heart of Darkness* and *Lord Jim* establishes
his frame on that same vision and begins to speak; with his moral
growth complete, Dowell falls silent.

The narrative and the central tale it relates interpenetrate in *The
Good Soldier* to a remarkable degree. As we saw in the last chapter,
something of the same is true in *Lord Jim*; Marlow garners new
testimony on Jim – from the French lieutenant, Stein, and others –
and adds each perspective to the tale. Like Dowell, who spends two
years making sense of his story, Jim's saga continues to expand for
Marlow, and some considerable time elapses between his evening's
talk in the darkness with a group of listeners and the letter that
arrives to complete the narrative for a solitary witness. What is
strikingly different in the two novels, however, is that Dowell's
understanding and new character continue to grow during the
years of wrestling with the stcry. We do not feel that Marlow has
changed as profoundly since first recognizing the irremediable
paradox apparent in Jim. His narration in *Lord Jim*, then, is a
response to a spiritual awakening already largely complete; it is the
performance of a role Marlow has newly fashioned for himself.
    In wandering with Dowell back and forth across the territory of
his memory, we are more intimately caught up in the slow
momentum through which he generates a new character and moral
perspective for himself. Testimony and events continue after the
tale has begun: Dowell's conversations off-stage with Leonora
Ashburnham, her eventual marriage to Rodney Bayham, and
Dowell's trip to Ceylon to retrieve Nancy Rufford are examples. Yet
none of these points of contact between the central story and the
narrative alters those events that led Dowell to speak in the first
place: his discovery of nine years of betrayal in his relations with the

Ashburnhams and the suicide of Edward Ashburnham. Rather, the two years it takes him to finish the tale, the events that occur during these years and, most important, the act of narration and the necessity of imposing pattern, all enable Dowell to come to terms with those first undeniable facts. He has changed, not they. Dowell articulates from the start his intention to use the narrative as a means of discovery and education.

> My wife and I knew Captain and Mrs. Ashburnham as well as it was possible to know anybody, and yet, in another sense, we knew nothing at all about them. This is, I believe, a state of things only possible with English people of whom, till today, when I sit down to puzzle out what I know of this sad affair, I knew nothing whatever.   (p. 3)

In making a story of his experience, he must puzzle out what he knows, generate pattern and sense for it. Until the moment he sits down to write he knew nothing. But with nearly his first written words he has claimed an initial insight, that with the English one can have long-standing relations and yet know only their public roles, nothing of the depths of their hearts.

The same process continues throughout the novel, giving the narrative its shape. Dowell's mind plays back and forth across the landscape of his memory, juxtaposing various scenes, characters, and events outside of a traditional linear concern with plot, the simple what-happened of the story. Thus, to an even greater degree than in *Lord Jim*, the narrative structure of *The Good Soldier* is determined by spatial form. Dowell's memory establishes the relations of elements of the story outside of a strictly temporal and causal sequence of action and reaction. Ford's well-known but typically vague expression for the strategy is the *progression d'effet*. Samuel Hynes, in perhaps the most important essay on the novel, claims that the narrative 'raises uncertainty about the nature of truth and reality to the level of a structural principle'.[4]

The strategy takes three distinct aspects in the narrative. The first is the repetition of a scene or event, each time with a greater sense of context or background in the reader's, as well as Dowell's, mind. An important example is an outing from Nauheim to the ancient city of M—, during which Florence Dowell draws along her husband and the Ashburnhams to a triumphant revelation of Luther's Protest. She turns to Edward Ashburnham: '"It's because of that piece of paper that you're honest, sober, industrious, provident, and clean-lived. If it weren't for that piece of paper you'd be like the Irish or the Italians or the Poles, but particularly the Irish". ... And she laid one hand upon Captain Ashburnham's wrist' (p. 44, Ford's ellipsis). Although the reader knows a good bit more at this stage than had Dowell, the full, complex ironies become apparent only as echoes of the scene return later. In Part Four, for instance, Dowell claims that what Leonora ought to have said, rather than revealing only the partial (and finally inconsequential) truth of her Irish Catholic faith, was: 'Your wife is a harlot who is going to be my husband's mistress ... ' (p. 191, Ford's ellipsis).

A second method that Dowell uses to give order, and through order meaning, to his experiences, is the simple juxtaposition of events, scenes, or characters without apparent causal relation: 'setting side by side details which do not naturally connect, and thus compelling in the reader an imaginative leap and resolution between them'.[5] On the train from Nauheim to M—, Dowell sees in a field 'a brown cow hitch its horns under the stomach of a black and white animal and the black and white one [is] thrown right into the middle of a narrow stream' (p. 42). No explicit link is necessary with the events to come.

The third method of spatial or thematic structuring most clearly establishes a parallel between Dowell's continuing search and re-creation of his memory, and the reader's own memory and reinterpretation of events that appeared early in the novel in light of later knowledge. Our interpretive struggle mirrors his. Dowell's nightmare image of divine judgment on Ashburnham and Florence includes a mysterious third figure. Our initial sense is that this must be Maisie Maiden; only much later do we finally realise that the 'poor girl' is Nancy Rufford.

> But upon an immense plain, suspended in mid-air, I seem to see three figures, two of them clasped close in an intense embrace, and one intolerably solitary. ... And the immense plain is the hand of God, stretching out for miles and miles, with great spaces above it and below it. And they are in the sight of God, and it is Florence that is alone. ...   (p. 70, first ellipsis mine, second Ford's)

The continuing interplay of Dowell's self-conscious memory with what it remembers – immediate, unreflective experience – is discussed from a phenomenological perspective by Paul

Armstrong.[6] What we know as 'personal identity' or character, a mature sense of self, is generated largely, Armstrong argues, by this same process of reflection on past experience. In a real sense, Dowell, before he brings himself to speak, has lacked some necessary element of individualized character. He seems to have been incapable of an interpretive detachment from either his on-going daily routine as an expatriate nursemaid or from the significant events in his own past. Yet with the manifold discoveries succeeding Edward Ashburnham's suicide such a detachment quickly develops as Dowell strives to understand. Armstrong suggests that 'Dowell's narration brings together both his unreflective experience and his self-conscious reflections. The action of his novel is the interaction of these two levels of intentionality.'[7] But Dowell's 'new awareness could not develop until his blind engagement with the world collapsed'.[8]

From out of the chaos of that collapse Dowell reaches towards an understanding of just what has happened and towards a new identity. The split between his present, self-conscious reflection and his first forty-five years is not temporal alone – the simple, on-going taking stock of where one is and where one has been. Rather, the abrupt detachment is akin to the sundering of an umbilical bond; all the assumptions, values, ideals on which Dowell has so contentedly secured himself have been shattered, have been pilloried. This profound break between the events of the central tale as Dowell lived them and the perspective through which he now labours to interpret, is what defines the structural irony of the frame narrative of *The Good Soldier*. Such irony colours and defines every one of his memories and re-evaluations, for it determines his attitude towards the entirety of his past. An essential distinction between the traditional frame narrative, such as in *Wuthering Heights* or *The Scarlet Letter*, and the novels considered in this study, lies in this ironic detachment between the narrator and his own past.

II

The damning aspect of Dowell's innocence before Ashburnham's suicide lies in another radical split within his character: between the conscious habits and values of his daily regimen and the unconscious desires he has so thoroughly repressed as to castrate himself.

In order to attain an integrity of character that will be the ground of a new moral vision, he must resolve this breach in his own soul.

Before the abrupt awakening to the reality of years of deception and betrayal, Dowell has sheltered himself within 'the secure and limited alternatives his society offers him', and were he not forced to 'look up from his path he [could] live out his life with a certain dull security'.[9] The norms of social behaviour, however, have offered more than simple shelter; Dowell's earlier selfhood seems to have been nearly identical with formal, empty rituals, neither more nor less than an embodiment of the Victorian–Edwardian social code. Indeed, Dowell may be judged as having lacked any meaningful identity whatsoever. In the tradition of nineteenth-century realism, as we saw earlier, fully realized character arose from 'the struggle between individual and social motives in the creation of meaning and interpretation. ... Worldly reality and individual temperament interact to stage the drama of character.'[10] Dowell so totally denies any personal desires, sexual or spiritual, that no such drama is possible.

A lack of realized or socialized character may be seen as common to the traditional frame narrative. *Wuthering Heights*, Turgenev's *First Love*, *The Scarlet Letter*, and Conrad's 'Youth' all relate a tale of youthful innocence or of a romantic figure's struggle against constraining social definition. Dowell, before his enlightenment, is certainly innocent as well. His is not, however, the vital, romantic innocence of youth, but self-imposed and distorting, denying both the needs of his own nature and the transgressions of others around him. His vague feelings of protest lead to not so much as a whine; they are overwhelmed with the necessity of living up to appearances.

> Mind, I am not saying that this is not the most desirable type of life in the world; that it is not an almost unreasonably high standard. For it is really nauseating, when you detest it, to have to eat every day several slices of thin, tepid, pink india rubber, and it is disagreeable to have to drink brandy when you would prefer to be cheered up by warm, sweet kummel. And it is nasty to have to take a cold bath in the morning when what you want is really a hot one at night. ...
>
> But these things have to be done; it is the cock that the whole of this society owes to Æsculapius.   (pp. 36–7)

Dowell's courtship of Florence exhibits little more passion than his resentment against unavoidable roast beef. Having met her at a New York party, he determines 'with all the obstinacy of a possibly weak nature, if not to make her [his], at least to marry her' (p. 78). At one moment on the night they elope, as Dowell later imagines, had he shown any warmth as she lay in his arms, she might later 'have acted the proper wife'. But because he 'acted like a Philadelphia gentleman' (p. 83), Florence pushes on with her scheme, feigning a bad heart as well as virginity, and cuckolding him through the years ahead.

Ford's indictment of this kind of radical disjunction between conscious social behaviour and unconscious desires (or private hypocrisy) figures throughout his career. One aspect of Christopher Tietjens' growth in *Parade's End* into what Norman Leer calls a 'limited hero'[11] is the re-integration of morally conscious behaviour and desire in his relations with Valentine Wannop. But John Dowell's passions are so thoroughly repressed that his nature is stunted and his vision distorted; he cannot see what the rest of the world acknowledges. Thus, in retrospect, he becomes a target for his narrative irony; relieved by Leonora's announcement after the scene in the castle of M— that she is Roman Catholic, he begs her to 'accept the situation' of friendly relations between the two couples. Leonora, having treated him from the beginning as if he and not Florence were the invalid – which is accurate enough – can only respond: '"Oh, I accept the situation," she said at last, "if you can"' (p. 68).

Dowell conceals from himself his own latent desires. He is, in other words, the agent of his own regulation and spiritual maiming. And as a husband he plays a similar role of censor, or attempts to, trying to keep Florence isolated from dangerous excitement.

> [M]y whole attentions, my whole endeavors were to keep poor dear Florence on to topics like the finds at Gnossos and the mental spirituality of Walter Pater. I had to keep her at it, you understand, or she might die.   (p. 16)

Through Dowell we see Ford's enmity, present in much of his pre-war fiction, towards Pater and the great 'men of ideas' of a generation earlier who 'were marked by their blindness to the real problems around them'.[12] The fragmentation of Dowell's character is a manifestation of what Ford saw as a broader cultural malaise. Of course, though he may succeed in dissociating his own conscious thoughts from unconscious impulse, Dowell is no more capable of regulating Florence's passions than is society. Those who are awakened to passion learn early, as do all the characters in *The Good Soldier* save Nancy and Dowell, to lead two lives: one of social propriety, one of private indulgence.

Spiritually lamed though he may be, Dowell does have passions and desires, though they are unconscious, nearly irretrievable. They become apparent to him only after the fact, when the safe, secure world he has known has already begun to fragment. His first response on learning of Florence's death is an unconsidered reflex: 'Now I can marry the girl' (p. 104). For some time he has been as deeply in love as he is able with Nancy Rufford, without daring to admit as much to himself.

> For I had never had the slightest conscious idea of marrying the girl; I never had the slightest idea even of caring for her. I must have talked in an odd way, as people do who are recovering from an anaesthetic. It is as if one had a dual personality, the one I being entirely unconscious of the other. I had thought nothing; I had said such an extraordinary thing.
>
> (p. 103)

Many of Dowell's characteristics are shared by Robert Grimshaw, the central character of *A Call*, Ford's most successful novel before *The Good Soldier*. A brief look at Grimshaw will begin to set Dowell in the larger context of Ford's fiction. Certainly Grimshaw is more aware than Dowell of his passions for two separate women. But for Grimshaw the smooth and dispassionate functioning of the social organism must take precedence, and he so little understands the depths of his own desires that he believes he can arrange the marriage of one of his loves, Pauline, to his best friend and then watch contentedly over them. Further, the girl Grimshaw has loved since they were both children, Katya Lascarides, refuses to marry him; she insists on living as a common law wife, as her mother had with her father. In the name of propriety Grimshaw refuses. Brought low at the end, however, and recognizing the terrible price he must pay for his conventions and his need to manipulate his feelings – and those of others, principally Pauline – Grimshaw capitulates to Katya's demands.

> I'm very tired; I'm very lonely. I've discovered that there are things one can't do – that I'm not the man I thought I was.

It's you who are strong and get what you want, and I'm only a meddler who muddles and spoils. That's the moral of the whole thing. Take me on your own terms and make what you can of me. I am too lonely to go on alone any more. I've come to give myself up.[13]

Grimshaw is a good man. Yet 'with his marked predilection for self-denial and social propriety, [he] typifies ... the English society ... which was marked by its inability to deal with situatitns involving passion by its much too strong concern for propriety'.[1] He is spiritually crushed, not by the two women, but by the basic disjunction of his reason and his desire, and by his inability to fathom himself. This sort of character, creative, potentially heroic, but doomed to a certain listless hysteria because of the demands of women and of flaws within his own soul, appears throughout Ford's early fiction. That this approximates Ford's vision of himself is evident from any number of sources. And this, in turn, should restrain us from dismissing Dowell at the outset as one 'who suffers from the madness of moral inertia'.[15]

One other earlier character, Don Kelleg in *An English Girl*, suggests even more strongly that Ford intended such figures as potentially heroic but circumscribed or lamed by a sordid, prosaic modern environment. Kelleg, like Dowell, is an expatriate American, earning his keep in London as an illustrator for magazines. He loathes everything that his father, an American business tycoon, stands for. On inheriting a fortune, he sets out for America to redress the wrongs by which the money was accrued. For all his noble intentions, however, Don Kelleg discovers himself ineffectual and powerless. He abhors the Coney Island values he discovers in America, those wronged by his father want neither his charity nor his pity, and the inheritance is so bound that he can receive the enormous income but not influence its sources.

Don is so sensitive, so attuned to the pain of others, that he is hardly capable of acting. He spends a great portion of the novel intending great deeds for moral ends and accomplishing little or nothing. His fiancée, Eleanor Greville, 'had had time to think that Don really *was* too self-conscious. A man *ought* not to be so much aware of his own mental attitudes. It was not exactly healthy'.[16]

More to the point, perhaps, is the verdict of Eleanor's father that the 'man's a poet: that's what the trouble is' (p. 235). With a poet's sensibility Don Kelleg observes, feels, judges. But he is not in step with the world; his values are not those of the modern spirit. He is torn by the dual impulse to retreat (as Dowell and Tietjens will finally do) and to immerse himself in the fray, which he does in the sudden, inexplicable conclusion to the novel as he leaves Eleanor behind and returns to America. Although less explicitly defeated than Robert Grimshaw, Kelleg, despite his poetic soul, never achieves the ironic detachment from the world and from his earlier self that Dowell will. Nevertheless, Ford clearly sees him as a romantic idealist, out of step with his time yet true to an older traditional system of values.

John Dowell's fragmentation of sensibilities, his passiveness and buried passion, his initial blindness to the external world and to parts of his own soul, all appear less idiosyncratic if we recognize his relation to other characters such as Grimshaw or Kelleg. Yet Dowell is not simply a more successful version of the same character. After his initial awakening to the sham of the social world and to unsuspected passions within himself, Dowell continues to grow and to act more meaningfully than either Grimshaw or Kelleg.

III

Although deeply divided within himself, Dowell's life had been superficially contented. But when Leonora lets him have the sordid facts 'full in the face' (p. 104), the shelter of ignorance is shattered. Dowell must face a moral chaos not centred in the external world, which runs smoothly enough from day to day, but within his own memory. This total moral disorientation is what he struggles to make sense of by telling a story. Before we examine Dowell's transformation of Ashburnham and his acceptance of Nancy Rufford, we must better understand his initial trauma.

The blow to Dowell's character caused by the multiple discoveries after Edward Ashburnham's death is more profound than the simple rage and humiliation of finding himself a cuckold. The dissolving of his illusions about the 'minuet de la cour' (p. 6) that lasted nine years dissolves as well the foundations of moral order on which his identity has rested. In *Heart of Darkness* Marlow journeys up the Congo, his identity flayed as he unearths the corruption of the colonial enterprise, a threatening wilderness without, and wild lusts within. In *Lord Jim*, the sight of Jim, guilty and romantically innocent, undermining Marlow's faith in a 'sovereign code of conduct', has the same impact. The setting of *The Good Soldier* is less exotic, the actions more decorous, but Dowell's character suffers an equivalent blow. When he claims that 'the death of a mouse from cancer is the whole sack of Rome by the Goths' (p. 5), the metaphor applies not only to the break up of a social unit, but to the turmoil besetting his own spirit. Like Rome he has fallen into a dark age without light, without value, without identity.

> And there is nothing to guide us. And if everything is so nebulous about a matter so elementary as the morals of sex, what is there to guide us in the more subtle morality of all other personal contacts, associations, and activities? Or are we meant to act on impulse alone? It is all a darkness. (p. 12)

Dowell's realisation that the conventions which have governed his life are both arbitrary and illusory carries with it a more severe reaction against society itself than does Marlow's. For although Marlow finds that the social world is rife with corruption and that the codes which bind men together are artifices, the struggle for renewed community remains the source of human values. The ideals that are the sinews of solidarity may be illusions, but they are in some sense necessary.

Throughout Conrad's early fiction the epitome of communities dependent for survival on the selflessness of its members is the merchant ship. In striking contrast, Dowell adopts the image of a ship to underscore not a necessary harmony but the bewildering inconsistency of appearance and reality.

> We were, if you will, one of those tall ships with the white sails upon a blue sea, one of those things that seem the proudest and the safest of all beautiful and safe things that God has permitted the mind of man to frame. Where better could one take refuge?
> (p. 6)

No sense of solidarity here – the illusion is a sham rather than a necessity. Rarely in Ford's fiction does community succour the human spirit. Society, rather, is the source of hypocrisy, betrayal, and, ironically, of acute personal isolation. The social relationship between the Dowells and the Ashburnhams was typically 'a prison – a prison full of screaming hysterics, tied down so that they might not outsound the rolling of our carriage wheels as we went along the shaded avenues of the Taunus Wald' (p. 7).

Blindness to the affairs of the world had determined the way
Dowell *saw*. The facts as he learns them at Branshaw, however,
radiate only a pervasive darkness. Yet the facts themselves appear
luminous, absolute, unchangeable. Florence had deceived him
since the first night of their marriage, and cuckolded him contin-
uously since not long thereafter. Edward Ashburnham, the good
soldier and gentleman, the paradigm of proper public behaviour,
has privately acted the 'raging stallion'. And Dowell, labouring to
make sense of it all, judges as he speaks, judges according to the
facts as he knows them.

As with Marlow and Jim, we have a narrator initially addressing
a character who seems to stand for the most profound breach
between appearance and reality, between the expectation of virtue
and the reality of ignominy. Dowell wrestles with Ashburnham's
'failure' (this verdict is later significantly muted, while for Jim it is
not), as a first, immediate step in regaining his equilibrium. If he
can find secure ground on which to *judge* Ashburnham, some sort
of moral order may yet be salvaged.

The first description of Ashburnham, the figure apparently at
the heart of duplicity, establishes the dichotomy between appearance and reality that will continue throughout the novel. At this
stage the story offers little sympathy for Ashburnham. His public
demeanour reveals a priggish 'touch of stupidity' (p. 8), while the
hidden reality is more sinister. 'You would have said that he was
just exactly the sort of chap that you could have trusted your wife
with. And I trusted mine – and it was madness' (p. 11). These first
sketch marks of Ashburnham's portrait are fleshed out during the
course of the narrative; the duration allows greater detail and, far
more important, the evolving portrait reflects the deepening of
Dowell's understanding and identification with the man.
Although Dowell traces what he believes must have been the
steady decline of Ashburnham's character during the years of his
marriage, what the portrait reveals is not significant change in
Ashburnham so much as a shift in Dowell's appraisal of him. The
Ashburnham who cuts his throat with a pen knife at the end is not
the same character who has just killed himself before Dowell
begins to tell that story. And this dynamic portrait, in turn,
represents Dowell's own growth. As he better understands
Ashburnham, the romantic idealism and the naivete, and the
forces that have slowly destroyed him, Dowell achieves an
education into the ways of man and the world.

The starting point of Dowell's moral growth is also the beginning of his attempt to puzzle out what he knows of the affair with the Ashburnhams. He has plunged from the comfortable routine of daily custom into a waste land of moral emptiness and loneliness. His sense of irony at the outset of the narrative is, in Kierkegaard's terms, *absolute*, slashing away all possibility of human value and communion.[17] Nothing redemptive is left of his former life or beliefs or world.

The beginning, for Dowell, is the word. He tentatively reaches out from the isolation, strives to understand and impose form on the chaos about him by speaking and making a story. Besides transforming private experience into history – a series of events in meaningful relation – his impulse is for purgation as well, to get the sight out of his head. Yet Dowell lacks Marlow's audience, even another solitary soul who has expressed concern. Without someone to acknowledge him, language and story seem meaningless, unshared, little more than a garbled shout. Thus Dowell projects a comfortable illusion *for himself*, an imaginary stage-set that will allow him to continue with the game.

> So I shall just imagine myself for a fortnight or so at one side of the fireplace of a country cottage, with a sympathetic soul opposite me. And I shall go on talking, in a low voice while the sea sounds in the distance and overhead the great black flood of wind polishes the bright stars. (p. 12)

Elsewhere in Ford's fiction we find similar retreats. In *An English Girl* Don Kelleg and Eleanor initially yearn for just this sort of hideaway before Kelleg's quixotic flight to America. Christopher Tietjens, in *Parade's End*, coming to recognize that his feudal sensibilities are anachronisms in post-war society, dreams of and finally succeeds in retreating to a country cottage with Valentine Wannop, there to survive by restoring and selling antiques – the life of what Ford calls the Small Producer – and to talk.

> You seduced a young woman in order to be able to finish your talks with her. You could not do that without living with her. You could not live with her without seducing her; but that was the by-product. The point is that you can't otherwise talk. You can't finish talks at street corners; in museums; even drawing-rooms. You mayn't be in the mood when she is in the mood – for the

intimate conversation that means the final communion of your souls. You have to wait together – for a week, for a year, for a lifetime, before the final intimate conversation may be attained ... .[18]

Tietjens succeeds in this self-transformation; for Dowell, however, no young woman waits poised to listen. Instead, the country cottage and his silent audience exist only in his imagination, further emphasizing his isolation. At the same time, the tale itself creates shelter and form opposed to the chaos of wind and darkness.

IV

Dowell's effort to resolve the deep division in his own nature is paralleled by his attempt to understand a similar paradox in Edward Ashburnham. Dowell comes to see the desperation that has driven Ashburnham in pursuit of women as an ironic distortion of the same ideals that once defined his behaviour as a landlord. He comes to portray Ashburnham as a romantic hero who has been destroyed, finally, by the oppressive norms of a modern social world which has no tolerance for his archaic sensibilities. Thus, the paradox of appearance and reality, of fidelity and betrayal in Ashburnham dissolves as he becomes more thoroughly Dowell's creation.

Almost immediately after our first glimpse of Ashburnham, so 'well set up ... such a touch of stupidity' (p. 8), and Leonora's revelation of her husband's infidelities, Dowell, with a full measure of irony, qualifies his judgment: 'I don't want you to think that I am writing Teddy Ashburnham down a brute' (p. 10). At this early stage, however, even Ashburnham's 'noble' qualities seem to Dowell as belonging to the realm of suspicious, treasonable appearance. The irony here further reflects the breach between appearance and reality. These are my words, Dowell seems to say, but their true meaning lies hidden; they are no more what they appear than is Teddy Ashburnham.

Whatever the falsehood of Ashburnham's propriety in Nauheim, Dowell discovers that in his other public role as landlord, actions and motives are clear, unambiguous, integral. As a responsible landholder Ashburnham's private longings and potentials are given structure by the socio-historical environment. Ashburnham has been bred, like Christopher Tietjens, for a specific function. He is responsible for the proper nurture of the land and its tenants. When times are prosperous their gain is his; when bad, 'everyone had to feel the pinch, landlord as well as tenants' (p. 145), as Ashburnham's land-steward tries to explain to Leonora. The reciprocal relationship engenders a harmony in keeping with a feudal world. Christopher Tietjens' role and identity are shattered by the war; much the same happens to Ashburnham when Leonora comes to Branshaw Teleragh. Her family have been impoverished Irish landholders, enduring ceaseless battles with their tenants. She has no way of fathoming her husband's sense of responsibility – that very element which gives his life meaning in addition to wealth – and she can only imagine that his excessive sentimentality will lead them to ruin.

Ashburnham's self-image has thus been founded on ideals that may be called feudal (as Ford would have it here and elsewhere in his fiction), or romantic, but which seem simply sentimental to Leonora and to society at large. Dowell himself repeatedly charges Ashburnham with sentimentality – his ironic tone acknowledging the trait as both blameworthy and noble. Duty and responsibility are clearly two of Ashburnham's guiding principles. Another, rather separate, is the nurturing love and devotion he believes that a woman owes her lord, and that a man must finally depend on for strength and balance.

> He imagined that no man can satisfactorily accomplish his life's work without the loyal and whole-hearted co-operation of the woman he lives with. (p. 146)

The source of this ideal may not be identical with that of the others – Dowell makes plain Ashburnham's fascination with novels of light romance. Nevertheless, an enduring, sentimental love is an integral part of the romantic image of life that Ashburnham pursues.

Although Dowell will attempt to translate Ashburnham's dream into his own life, he himself never directly questions this relation between Ashburnham's inherited role and his yearning for an ideal love. Whether such a love is necessary to fulfilling the character Ashburnham has been bred to assume, or is an in-born element of his imagination, or is simply the product of sentimental fiction remains unaddressed. This will heighten, in turn, the pathos and irony of Dowell's own situation at Branshaw after he has accepted responsibility for both the estate and Nancy Rufford.

The vagueness of the relationship between the ideals of social responsibility and personal love reflects a deep ambivalence towards passion on Ford's own part. Throughout his fiction (and clearly his life as well),[19] romantic love represents both the life's-blood of human communion and of equally profound human weakness and vulnerability. Robert Grimshaw is crushed by his failure to comprehend or control his passions; yet Christopher Tietjens' self-creation as a Small Producer is possible only with the acceptance of his feelings for Valentine Wannop. Though not at the ancient estate of Groby –Tietjens having forsworn that anachronistic burden – Valentine performs much the same function of loving support that Ashburnham longs for. In *The Good Soldier* we may well feel that Ashburnham's desire for his woman to share spiritually his proprietorship of the land and to nurture him is in keeping with the harmony of such pastoral life. Leonora's lack of sympathetic understanding may well represent an emotional narrowness on her part. At the same time, however, when Ashburnham turns away from Leonora – to the point, finally, of abrogating his role at Branshaw – and seeks the good will of other women, he gives way to weakness and folly, at the cost of losing something of himself. This is a self-betrayal similar to the division of conscious behaviour and desire in Dowell. For one man this self-maiming leads to a series of unfulfilling or humiliating affairs; for the other it robs him of passion altogether.

The breach between Ashburnham and Leonora drives him step by step further away from Branshaw and his natural element and into a world that assaults the traditional foundations of his character. He becomes the dissembling creature that so confounds Dowell. The ideals of Ashburnham's self-image at Branshaw are little more than the external trappings of proper behaviour by the time he arrives in Nauheim. His pursuit of ideal love and feminine understanding forces him into deceit and humiliation. As he gradually becomes less capable of meaningful action – his first tempestuous affair with the courtesan La Dolciquita having cost him control of Branshaw Teleragh – Ashburnham seeks women who will talk to him of the ideals he has in some sense forsaken:

> [T]here were quite a number of ladies in his set who were capable of agreeing with this handsome and fine fellow that the duties of a feudal gentleman were feudal. ... He wanted only moral support at the hands of some female, because he found men difficult to talk to about ideals.   (p. 158)

One characteristic trait that survives in Ashburnham throughout, however, is his sense of responsibility. This is the feature that Dowell finds most admirable, at the last truly heroic, and Dowell will adopt it as central to his own new character. At Branshaw such responsibility is in keeping with the role Ashburnham performs. Later, as an officer travelling aboard ship with his troops through the Red Sea, he twice leaps overboard to rescue men maddened by heat and sun. Again Leonora can react only with disheartened rage. She hates 'his deeds of heroism' (p. 171). Yet for Edward these men are his charges, and to act otherwise would be to betray himself.

The same impulse, however, when combined with Ashburnham's quest for an ideal love, renders him both vulnerable to women and absurd. He believes he has wronged each of the women who have yielded themselves up to him, and he insists on assuming responsibility for them. With some, such as Mrs Basil, the consequences are not great, simply periodic 'loans' to disingenuous husbands. La Dolciquita, however, wants more tangible rewards.

> He tried to convince this woman, who, as he saw it, had surrendered to him her virtue, that he regarded it as in any case his duty to provide for her, and to cherish her and even to love her – for life. (p. 161)

Having got what was to be had, La Dolciquita mercifully throws Ashburnham out. Florence Dowell is less kind. She demands of him precisely the endless devotion he had offered the other woman years earlier. As Leonora recognizes, his affair with Florence is a final degradation. His passion for her, intense though it may initially be, has no more substance than the challenge of a polo match. Mercenary, shallow if well educated, her imagination guileful rather than romantic, Florence could never be the woman to make Ashburnham himself again.

When Ashburnham has been driven furthest from himself, enduring the shrill insistencies near and far of Florence for nine years, having no real communication with his wife, the two surviving noble traits of his character – his sense of personal responsibility and his yearning for an ideal, fulfilling love – come directly into conflict. He falls in love with Nancy Rufford.

The girl has been the Ashburnhams' ward since she was a child. And she worships Edward – he has been to her 'the model of humanity, the hero, the athlete, the father of his country, the law-giver' (p. 112). For Nancy Rufford, Ashburnham exists as that same idealized image he has pursued all these years. She is not simply another sympathetic soul willing to listen to him; unlike Leonora, she shares the stuff of his imagination. For her, Ashburnham is 'Lohengrin and the Cid in one body' (p. 90).

As with Dowell's continuing use of the narrative to understand himself and to make sense of his experience, speech reveals to Ashburnham his own passion for the girl. He swears to Dowell that until he first declared his love in the Casino of Nauheim, he had 'regarded her exactly as he would have regarded a daughter' (p. 111). It is not simply that in speaking Ashburnham stumbles on his own hidden emotions; as Dowell interprets the event, those emotions are partly created by the words that express them.

> It was as if his passion for her hadn't existed; as if the very words that he spoke, without knowing that he spoke them, created the passion as they went along. Before he spoke, there was nothing; afterwards, it was the integral fact of his life.   (p. 116)

Ashburnham's night-long confession to Dowell anticipates what the other will do in turn – make a story of his experience and tell his tale to a silent audience, 'a woman or a solicitor' (p. 250), as if to make it real, to have it exist independently of his own thoughts. At another remove this is similar to the process we use in constructing an interpretive response to the novel. Ashburnham makes a story of his life – an argument – as does Dowell; we make a story of our experience of that story. In this way we fashion a psychological framework for understanding the novel. The elements, paradoxes, characters of the story become meaningful as they are integrated into that framework. This is especially true in such a novel as *The Good Soldier* in which events, situations, and characters strike resonances and demand reappraisals across the boundaries of a traditional, linear plot.

Ashburnham is adept at the task, though the form he gives his tale is, in keeping with his sensibility, shaped according to the sentimental conventions of light romance. He, like Jim, can still trust in the straightforward meaning of a story that has developed through time from one event to the next.

> [T]he fellow talked like a cheap novelist. – Or like a very good novelist for the matter of that, if it's the business of a novelist to

make you see things clearly. And I tell you I see that thing as clearly as if it were a dream that never left me.   (p. 109)

For Ford, Conrad, and other literary impressionists, this ability to render an event or character so clearly as to be seen is the primary artistic endeavour.[20] Dowell never reports Ashburnham's precise words, but like him seeks to evoke a vivid immediacy.

The love for Nancy that Ashburnham unearths in his own words immediately comes into conflict with his code of personal responsibilities. The words have escaped an unconscious source. Otherwise 'he would have fled from it as from a thing accursed' (p. 111). He has been *responsible* for her. She has been his ward, as dependent on him as any creature of Branshaw. To violate that care, that responsibility, even in satisfying at last a deep yearning, would be to destroy the integrity of his romantic ideals and image of himself – the image Nancy herself adores until later poisoned by Leonora's machination. With that Leonora finally shatters the ratifying mirror of all that Ashburnham has aspired to.

Ashburnham affirms the love by sacrificing himself to it. And the sacrifice is in the name of duty and responsibility as well. Strikingly, therefore, at the same time that the internal struggle pits Asburnham against himself, it also re-integrates his character. The romantic ideals of love and responsibility, which have been largely forsaken during his purgatorial years of yearning and self-deceit, are brought to the test, and he remains faithful to both. Ashburnham forbids himself the love that, in different circumstances, a different world, would make him whole. It is Dowell who tells, as an act of love, Ashburnham's story and at last fashions him as a romantic hero.

V

Love and responsibility, the ideals of Ashburnham's character, have never much mattered to Dowell – they have been abstract notions only as real to him as his marriage. As his understanding of Ashburnham deepens, so does his appreciation of these fundamental human values. The radical irony that marked his tone at the start, undercutting all meaning and values, slowly evolves on the same course as his moral education, to embrace both a scepticism towards society at large and the redemptive significance of love and responsibility. When Dowell acts to fulfil these ideals, though in a small and circumscribed way, he will merit the status of hero.

At almost the exact centre of the narrative, Dowell discloses his love for Nancy Rufford, first declared to Leonora the same night as his wife's death and only hours after Ashburnham has spoken to the girl of his own passion. What follows, however, is no paean to Dowell's love, but his attempt to fathom and articulate Ashburnham's behaviour, and a discourse on the nature of man's love for woman. This section represents the first significant clue to Dowell's gradual moral development. The change is manifest in his perception of paradox in Ashburnham's nature; no longer is the issue simply one of appearance and reality – of the superficial behaviour of a gentleman and the appetites of a raging stallion – indeed, the coin has been reversed. Ashburnham's apparent guilt as a seducer and hypocrite, which Dowell was brought to see by Leonora, conceals or coexists with an undeniable nobility of spirit. While his sudden confession of passion to the girl may be the 'most monstrously wicked thing Edward Ashburnham ever did in his life' (p. 113), Dowell nevertheless can no longer think of him 'as anything but straight, upright, and honourable' (p. 113). No irony undercuts this statement as it had earlier. Rather, Dowell's appraisal of Ashburnham's character represents his own changing view of the world: that such paradox is unavoidable, that honourable action and love do achieve meaning in the face of a corrupt society, though they may finally be destroyed by it.

Only in passing does Dowell mention his own love for Nancy Rufford; this is not his story, he contends, and his feelings bear so very little on what 'happens'. Yet in trying to explain Ashburnham's love for the girl, and then moving to a general discourse on the subject, Dowell demonstrates that he too is learning to love. Never has he claimed that he once loved Florence – merely that he was determined to marry her. Whatever physical passion he may have felt for her or Leonora or other women has been repressed to the point of extinction. Even after discovering his love for Nancy, Dowell seems baffled by the fact. In telling the story, in wrestling with Ashburnham and the others, however, he has learned enough to speak of love with confidence and intimacy.

Ashburnham loved Nancy Rufford – did so, Dowell believes, as he had no one else: 'she was the only woman he ever really loved' (p. 113). The intensity of this love, and the fact that Ashburnham was willing to sacrifice himself to it while not pursuing it – rising above the sort of weakness that characterized his earlier passions – stands for Dowell as an affirmation of human communion and meaning. He now sees love, rather than as a matter of proper social constellations on the one hand and of lust and betrayal on the other, as an 'alleviation, however precarious, of basic anxiety, and as a renewal of the feeling that one's very existence may have justification'.[21]

Although Dowell is explicitly attempting to comprehend Ashburnham's relationship with the girl, his quest for understanding drifts into more abstract considerations, revealing more of his own nature than at any other moment in the narrative. That he too has loved Nancy he knows; yet only in the effort to articulate the impulse and the need of Ashburnham does Dowell begin to fathom himself.

> But the real fierceness of desire, the real heat of a passion long continued and withering up the soul of a man, is the craving for identity with the woman he loves. He desires to see with the same eyes, to touch with the same sense of touch, to hear with the same ears, to lose his identity, to be enveloped, to be supported. For, whatever may be said of the relation of the sexes, there is no man who loves a woman that does not desire to come to her for the renewal of his courage, for the cutting asunder of his difficulties. And that will be the mainspring of his desire for her. We are all so afraid, we are all so alone, we all so need from the outside the assurance of our own worthiness to exist. (p. 115)

Already the process of Dowell's identification with Ashburnham is well underway. For though Dowell speaks of these as universal truths, he is interpreting Ashburnham and revealing himself.

As the narrative nears its end, Dowell repeats at several points his new found identification with Edward Ashburnham, believing that they share some essential quality of imagination and romantic idealism which cuts them off from the Leonoras and Rodney Bayhams.

> For I can't conceal from myself the fact that I loved Edward Ashburnham – and that I love him because he was just myself. ... He seems to me like a large elder brother who took me out on several excursions and did many dashing things whilst I

just watched him robbing the orchards, from a distance.

(pp. 253–4)

Dowell's ability to love Ashburnham and Nancy Rufford is, as Samuel Hynes suggests, 'his finest and most saving attribute'.[22] But the capacity is one not readily apparent in his earlier life, nor even as he picks up his pen; it is one he discovers and develops along the way.

When Dowell claims that Ashburnham was just himself, he affirms more than a spiritual brotherhood. For Ashburnham, the doomed romantic hero of the last pages of *The Good Soldier*, is thoroughly a creature of the narrative, given unity by the process of spatial juxtaposition, and transformed by Dowell's imagination. Dowell has fashioned an Ashburnham who will fit that same ideal image he, Ashburnham, had apparently dreamed of. Earlier in the novel Dowell asks, 'For who in this world can give anyone a character? Who in this world knows anything of any other heart – or of his own?' (p. 155) The 'historical' Ashburnham, eighteen months dead, is not given character by Dowell – a new Ashburnham has been created.

The measure of change in Dowell's judgment of Ashburnham can also be seen in the full turn of his ironic tone. Rather than the repeated assertion that Ashburnham was a 'good soldier', undercut by the brittle irony of disabused bitterness, by the end Dowell is ready to claim that the 'villains – for obviously Edward and the girl were villains – have been punished by suicide and madness' (p. 252). Here the irony simultaneously mocks social standards of judgment (which Dowell had earlier shared) and establishes Ashburnham and Nancy as something quite other than villains. Indeed, the absolute and clearly ironical term *villain* guides the reader's reconstruction of an alternative meaning to an opposite extreme. In Dowell's eyes, therefore, the essential truth of Ashburnham's character lies in this single absolute contradiction to society's comfortable verdict. The earlier apparent paradoxes of appearance and reality, of simultaneous virtue and vice, have disappeared. Ashburnham has become an integrated character, a romantic hero brutalized by a hostile environment.

Dowell's allegiance with villains who have threatened the equanimity of society reveals the significant change in his own character as well. His embracing of Ashburnham represents a rejection of the social world and its codes – all that had formerly given his life structure. Instead, his new moral identity is founded on those elements of his own nature he has discovered while telling the tale – principally his capacity for love – on the romantic ideals he has adopted from Ashburnham, and on a radical scepticism towards modern society.

> Society must go on, I suppose, and society can only exist if the normal, if the virtuous, and the slightly deceitful flourish, and if the passionate, the headstrong, and the too-truthful are condemned to suicide and madness. But I guess that I myself, in my fainter way, come into the category of the passionate, of the headstrong, of the too-truthful.   (p. 253)

Dowell's moral growth and his emergence as a heroic figure are predicated on this paradoxical awareness. Yet this perspective of general irony isolates Dowell at the end of *The Good Soldier* to much the same degree he had earlier been isolated by his own blindness, self-deception, and impotence. Once again he is charged with the care of a woman, Nancy Rufford, who cannot love him. In accepting this responsibility he affirms a final tie with Ashburnham, who also insisted on assuming responsibility for the women he loved. And they have both loved this woman. More than that, Dowell has *chosen*. Having judged the rabbit-like world of Leonora and Rodney Bayham, of normality and intolerance, he has rejected it and chosen to retreat to Branshaw Teleragh and be nursemaid to Nancy. The situation is grotesque – not yet in Ford's fiction can the retreat be, as in *Parade's End*, both a rejection of the modern world and a positive alternative to it. Nevertheless, Dowell has acted, heroically, according to imperatives of responsibility and of love, for Nancy Rufford as well as for Edward Ashburnham.

Yet despite identifying with the Ashburnham he has created, Dowell is no romantic hero. Like Marlow and our other narrators, he lacks a vital immediacy, an ability to plunge impulsively into his dream and to act in the world. His irony now, rather than his blindness, distances him from his past and from the social world. He must imagine watching his romantic hero robbing orchards in the distance. Yet it is also this ironic awareness that lets him *see*. And that, for Ford, is a heroic achievement: to learn to see by telling the tale – and to have told that tale.

4

Within and Without: Nick Carraway

I

I was within and without, simultaneously enchanted and repelled by the inexhaustible variety of life.[1]

That Nick Carraway supersedes his own creation, Jay Gatsby, as hero of *The Great Gatsby* is no starting revelation.[2] Yet despite their imaginative bond, they are very different sorts of hero. For Nick's achievement is subtle and complex, accomplishing what Gatsby cannot – sustaining a dream – while both recognizing the limitations of that dream and judging the social world that has destroyed it. A synthesis of disparate impulses whose roots lie in nineteenth-century romanticism and realism, Nick's heroism is borne out in his assuming responsibility for Gatsby and in the act of narration.

Once again, the narrative is shaped by a perspective of general irony which also marks Nick's moral maturity. Unlike John Dowell and to a greater degree than Marlow, however, Nick Carraway possesses a formidable ironic sensibility from the start. For he has already lost something of his innocence in the Great War, anticipating the fuller disillusionment we shall find in *The Sun Also Rises* and lacking in the earlier, pre-war novels. Yet this characteristic detachment is qualitatively different from his later one of general irony. Some part of Carraway's self-consciousness typically stands aloof from any immediate situation, observing and judging. Rarely does he lose himself in the welter of life.

Arthur Mizener considers this trait of immersion and detachment to be among Fitzgerald's own habitual attitudes: 'At its best, his mind apprehended things simultaneously with a participant's vividness of feeling and an intelligent stranger's acuteness of observation.'[3] In *The Great Gatsby*, Nick acknowledges this characteristic at the outset, citing the advice of his father.

I'm inclined to reserve all judgments, a habit that has opened up
many curious natures to me and also made me the victim of not a
few veteran bores. ... Reserving judgments is a matter of infinite
hope. I am still a little afraid of missing something if I forget that, as
my father snobbishly suggested, and I snobbishly repeat, a sense
of the fundamental decencies is parcelled out unequally at birth.

(p. 7)

This advice comes from the vantage of the narrative frame. Nick
addresses the reader directly, outside of the context and the
boundaries of the tale he is about to tell. More than establishing a
background for understanding Nick, this passage helps fashion an
appropriate reader for the novel. It explicitly directs us to make
sense of the story by sharing the same virtue; it urges on the reader
a similar critical detachment and suspension of judgment. As
with so many of its influences on *Gatsby*,[4] the narrative frame of
Conrad's *Heart of Darkness* performs a similar function. Marlow
recounts his tale on board the *Nellie* to men who share sensibilities
related to their 'bond of the sea'. As I argue in Chapter 1, the
primary narrator draws the reader into the privy circle and shapes
his understanding according to its sensibilities.

In *The Great Gatsby* the reader's critical duties must begin, of
course, with evaluating Nick himself. The smug and self-satisfied
claims of these opening pages have led some critics to attack
Carraway's reliability as narrator:[5] how far, the question must be
asked, are we to trust his interpretations of events and, when he
comes to make them, his judgments? The question remains open
to the end when our experience of the novel as a whole leads us not
simply to accept Nick's reliability, but his heroism as well.

Nick seems aware of the pretentiousness in these opening
pages; he invites the reader to begin judging him here at the outset,
to recognize the foundation of his strength – a deeply rooted code
of behaviour – as well as his limitations. His inconsistencies, even
his moderate failures, do not undermine his reliability, far from it;
they point out that he, like the rest, is a fallible creature in a flawed
environment. As Thomas Hanzo says of Nick, 'his irregularities of
behavior, his carelessness, do not escape his judgment; he does
not grow more confused but learns to see more clearly what
Eastern society and morality are and how he has been corrupted by
them'.[6]

Learning to see, as with Marlow and Dowell, involves a radical
redefinition of character, a profound moral education. And this is
the story Nick tells. The Carraway who arrives on Long Island in

search of fortune is very different from the Carraway who recounts the tale. A transformation has occurred; with the naive, complacent assumptions of youth shaken from him, Nick has had to fashion a new moral identity for himself. As we shall see, the foundation for this self-creation (and for his creation of Jay Gatsby as a romantic hero), will once more be a perspective of general irony.

Nick's achievement can be contrasted with those characters of nineteenth-century realism whose maturity synthesizes hidden desires and potentials with the conventions of the socio-historical environment. After their difficult, often painful educations, figures such as Rastignac and Pip are prepared to take their places in society as characters whose duty is meaningful, moral action. Whatever they have lost along the way, whatever innocence or faith, they have gained much. Fitzgerald's fiction charts a similar journey. His stories and novels are centrally concerned with the passage from innocence to some awareness of mature experience. What marks his work off from traditional realism, however, is the romantic despair penetrating the tone and structure of his stories: his characters often lose more than they gain. Their maturity involves a loss of more than innocence – of a spiritual vitality which, once gone, can never be replenished. Just beyond this stage, moreover, lies a region where so much vitality has been dissipated that life is listless, hardly endurable. Mizener details how abiding a fear this 'Emotional Bankruptcy' was in Fitzgerald's life. And in his fiction it was 'the most pervasive idea he ever had and it derives directly from his own knowledge of himself'.[7]

For Fitzgerald, youth is not so much a time of ignorance, as of charged expectancy. Amory Blaine in *This Side of Paradise*, Dexter Green in 'Winter Dreams', George O'Kelly in 'The Sensible Thing', and Basil Duke Lee in 'Basil and Cleopatra', all yearn for a chance to test themselves, to project their wills on a world whose malleable stuff lies waiting for engagement. In each case the abrupt focus of these wild yearnings is a beautiful, rich, devil of a girl. As Gatsby will discover as a young officer in Louisville, life is at its most intense, closest to ecstatic fulfilment when all of the stored energy and innocence and raw possibility of youth are first concentrated on such a girl. The intensity of initial courtship itself has the rhythm of consummation, regardless of what physical acts may occur.

The price of this excitement, and of pursuing still more, however, is high; such a plateau cannot be sustained. Each of these young men fails, at least initially, to win his girl. Failure expends personal vitality and slowly destroys ideals and illusions. In these stories it seems that the courtship patterns of society leech the life of youth, as if to sustain itself. 'The Sensible Thing' is representative.

George O'Kelly, having managed a financial miracle, returns to Tennessee to claim his prize, Jonquil Cary, only to discover that much has been lost. As Gatsby will Daisy, George has transformed the girl he loves into a creature of his own imagination, a vague goal towards which he has bent all of his energy and desire. Yet the girl herself can hardly appreciate his achievement. And the right moment for them has passed; they sit awkwardly, aware that their earlier passion has vanished – though it seems that Jonquil, as disillusioned as he, is nevertheless content to resume their affair. The loss, however, remains.

On that sofa he had felt agony and grief such as he would never feel again. He would never be so weak or so tired and miserable and poor. Yet he knew that that boy of fifteen months before had had something, a trust, a warmth that was gone forever.[8]

The normal course of things brings about the momentary blossoming of youth's dreams on the face of a seductive universe. The instant passes; the dream fades; George and Dexter and Basil are adults. Their characters are moulded by the conflict of their imaginations with an indifferent, if not tryannous social world. They lack the consolation of nineteenth-century realism that they will be fulfilled as mature players in the social drama.

The greater scope of *This Side of Paradise* led Fitzgerald, especially in revision of the original version, to reach beyond the simple despair of disillusioned youth towards some fuller notion of mature experience and ambition. Amory Blaine passes through not one but two similar experiences with women. The first with Isabelle in what had been the original novel, 'The Romantic Egotist', leads to little significant growth. After his short dream-like passion for Eleanor in 'Book Two: The Education of a Personage', however, Amory's loss of innocence propels him on in the rough mimicking of a traditional novel of education. Yet despite his self-conscious literary allusions, Amory never gains a markedly new sensibility. He discovers only vague desires to write and to give people a 'sense of security' (p. 241).

> Amory was alone – he had escaped from a small enclosure into a great labyrinth. He was where Goethe was when he began 'Faust'; he was where Conrad was when he wrote 'Almayer's Folly'.[9]

The structure of *This Side of Paradise* thus anticipates Nick Carraway's education and transformation, though little in Amory bears out equally profound change. Amory's attempts at irony towards the end of the novel display neither Nick's self-awareness nor a broader sense of irony and paradox, but rather a postured cynicism, contemptuous of the poor, disillusioned with the wealthy.

While many elements of the pattern of love and disillusioned maturity in the early stories are repeated in *The Great Gatsby*, in crucial ways both Carraway and Gatsby are exceptions to it. Gatsby quite simply refuses diminution of his dream. Without such admission, no significant compromise of character, no synthesis of private impulses and social conventions, is possible. And Nick's maturity as narrator, his newly generated character, is of a different order than that of Dexter or George or Amory. He is a decade older than they, and it is unclear whether he has himself ever endured an overwhelming passion. Yet his experience during the central tale of *Gatsby* does represent a related process: his new moral sensibility arises from the clash of his private values with the brutally indifferent waste land that destroys Gatsby. Not the failure of passion for a woman, therefore, but the defeat of a romantic figure whom, finally, he has partly created as well as bound himself to transforms Nick.

II

We have already noted that as a character in the central tale Nick possesses a self-conscious detachment from any situation in which he finds himself. His narrative irony, however, has a far broader reach, representing the moral perspective he achieves during the course of his experience with Gatsby. Within any given scene both forms are in play: the immediate ironies of words, gestures, or events, and the over-arching irony that fits that scene into the larger shape and concerns of the novel. Nick, in one instance, is dragged to the apartment where Tom Buchanan and Myrtle Wilson act out their romance. Myrtle's sister, Catherine, eagerly expains why the affair remains only an affair.

> 'It's really his wife that's keeping them apart. She's a Catholic and they don't believe in divorce.'
> Daisy was not a Catholic, and I was a little shocked at the elaborateness of the lie. (p. 34.)

Nick, aware of pertinent details, recognizes and is shocked by the irony of words that betray such unquestioning belief in Tom's good faith. Yet the full significance of Catherine's statement can only be glimpsed in terms of larger ironies of faith and faithlessness in the novel. This structural irony 'stands back' from the whole of the story as Nick stands back from this 'squalid scene'.

> I wanted to get out and walk eastward toward the park through the soft twilight, but each time I tried to go I became entangled in some wild, strident argument which pulled me back, as if with ropes, into my chair. Yet high over the city our line of yellow windows must have contributed their share of human secrecy to the casual watcher in the darkening streets, and I was him too, looking up and wondering. I was within and without, simultaneously enchanted and repelled by the inexhaustible variety of life.
> (p. 36)

As a character, Nick is immersed and detached from the immediate scene, and 'simultaneously enchanted and repelled' by life. These contradictory impulses anticipate the fuller paradox of his narrative perspective on events, of his sense of general irony. He will affirm the value of fundamental decencies while recognizing that the modern world disdains them. He will create Gatsby as a romantic hero, though well aware of Gatsby's own internal contradictions.

Carraway's moral growth is, indeed, most evident in the changing of his attitude towards Gatsby. Within the action of the story, Nick's judgment varies dramatically from moment to moment as he confronts the contradiction apparent in Gatsby. As narrator, however, Nick is able to comprehend these paradoxes.

And his first mention of Gatsby comes in fact from the vantage of the narrative frame.

> When I came back from the East last autumn I felt that I wanted the world to be in uniform and at a sort of moral attention forever; I wanted no more riotous excursions with privileged glimpses into the human heart. Only Gatsby, the man who gives his name to this book, was exempt from my reaction – Gatsby, who represented everything for which I have an unaffected scorn. If personality is an unbroken series of successful gestures, then there was something gorgeous about him, some heightened sensitivity to the promises of life. ...   (p. 8)

Here Nick can accept, can nearly celebrate both Gatsby's inherent contradictions and his own paradoxical attitude towards him. As he speaks, the experience lies already behind, and his moral growth is largely complete.

During most of the action of the central tale, however, Nick's attitude towards Gatsby vacillates explosively from admiration and allegiance to disdain and repulsion. As Gatsby drives Nick into the city, for example, recounting his 'life-story' in hope of squelching wild rumours, he rambles on about a mysterious sadness, about his war-time heroics; Nick recoils with suppressed laughter. His characteristic sense of irony erupts at this series of cliches stolen from 'a dozen magazines' (p. 62). But Gatsby pulls an authentic-looking medal from his pocket, along with a photo of himself at Oxford. Nick impulsively throws off his earlier doubts and accepts the whole of it:

> Then it was all true. I saw the skins of tigers flaming in his palace on the Grand Canal; I saw him opening a chest of rubies to ease, with their crimson-lighted depths, the gnawing of his broken heart.   (p. 62)

What irony we sense in the tone here is directed no longer at Gatsby but by Nick as narrator at his own earlier impulsive credulity.

The same sort of violent shift in judgment occurs after Myrtle's death. Nick initially assumes that Gatsby is doubly responsible: for hitting her and then for running. And when he discovers Gatsby attentively waiting outside the Buchanans' house in the night, he claims that it 'seemed a despicable occupation. For all I knew he was going to rob the house in a moment' (p. 127). Yet when Nick gathers the truth – that Daisy was driving – he reconnoitres the house himself on Gatsby's behalf, and urges him to 'come home and get some sleep' (p. 129). Nick's faith will not waver again. By the next day the profound change in his own character has emerged. Something in Gatsby's failure and the collapse of his dream have awakened Nick to the corruption of Eastern society, to the enduring value of human decency, and to his own sympathetic bond with Gatsby's romantic imagination. As he leaves, Carraway distances himself from the standards of the 'rotten crowd' and allies himself finally with Gatsby. This moment marks the culmination of Nick's moral journey and the commencement of his heroic responsibility.

> We shook hands and I started away. Just before I reached the hedge I remembered something and turned around.
> 'They're a rotten crowd,' I shouted across the lawn. 'You're worth the whole damn bunch put together.'
> I've always been glad I said that. It was the only compliment I ever gave him, because I disapproved of him from beginning to end.   (p. 136)

Again Nick as narrator insists on the irremediable paradox of Gatsby's character. He may be better than all the rest, but Nick disapproves of his egoism and corruption. Nevertheless, Nick Carraway's general irony comprehends the paradox without attempting the distortion of 'resolving' it.

III

The distinction between character and personality suggested from the earliest pages of *The Great Gatsby* reveals just how fully Gatsby as a romantic hero is Nick's creation. Character as defined by Nick is essentially private; personality appears in public performance. This is an important reversal of the realist tradition I discussed earlier, in which character – the fullest realization of an individual – lies precisely in the public, historical interplay of private impulses and social conventions. But in *The Great Gatsby* an individual's essential qualities remain forever hidden. Fitzgerald makes it clear that to know another person in any substantial way lies somewhere

between a leap of imaginative faith and the sheerly impossible.
Dowell's education in *The Good Soldier* included a similar lesson –
having been so monumentally wrong in his evaluations of others
around him, he comes to ask, 'For who in this world can give
anyone a character?'[10] Nevertheless, just as Dowell continues his
labour of understanding Ashburnham, Carraway's entire relationship with Gatsby depends on his efforts to translate the mysterious
man's dramatic gestures into a revelation of their hidden significance:

> If personality is an unbroken series of successful gestures, then
> there was something gorgeous about him, some heightened
> sensitivity to the promises of life.   (p. 8)

Nick's interpretive imagination is thus at work from the outset. The
conditional 'if' emphasizes the process; on to a skeleton of public
gestures Nick fleshes a Gatsby, someone whose essential romantic
hopefulness is expressed in his behaviour. Were any other figure in
the novel to tell his story, to interpret the same gestures, however,
Gatsby might well appear as a bootlegger living under an alias on
Long Island, rather than the romantic hero we in fact encounter.
   Much the same creative, interpretive impulse operates between
other characters in the novel; Gatsby himself transforms Daisy's
calculated dance – her everlasting freshness and gaiety, the music
and extravagance of her voice – into the object of his dream. As our
relation to Gatsby is mediated by Nick, so our perspective on Daisy
is divided, with Gatsby performing as a narrator of her splendour,
while Nick provides a less enchanted estimation. Marius Bewley
makes a similar point:

> Daisy Buchanan exists at two well-defined levels in the novel.
> She is what she is – but she exists at the level of Gatsby's vision of
> her.[11]

It is important to add that even what Daisy 'is' emerges only
through Nick's own private interpretation.
   The dilemma for characters to interpret each other's gestures –
and, just as important, the concurrent dilemma of the uncertain
relation between public gesture and inner 'truth' – occurs throughout Fitzgerald's fiction. Rosemary Hoyt, in *Tender is the Night*, falls in
love with the carefully fashioned persona of Dick Diver, a persona

that is the most ironic manifestation of the self-betrayal that rules his life.

As Fitzgerald's characters struggle to fathom each other, nevertheless, they must trust in a faithful relation between personality and character. Yet early in *The Great Gatsby* Daisy demonstrates that no such harmony is necessary. Sitting with Nick on the front porch of her house, she makes a grand and fashionable speech of disillusion.

'You see I think everything's terrible anyhow,' she went on in a convinced way. 'Everybody thinks so – the most advanced people. And I *know*. I've been everywhere and seen everything and done everything.' Her eyes flashed around her in a defiant way, rather like Tom's, and she laughed with thrilling scorn. 'Sophisticated – God, I'm sophisticated!'

The instant her voice broke off, ceasing to compel my attention, my belief, I felt the basic insincerity of what she had said. It made me uneasy, as though the whole evening had been a trick of some sort to exact a contributory emotion from me. I waited, and sure enough, in a moment she looked at me with an absolute smirk on her lovely face, as if she had asserted her membership in a rather distinguished secret society to which she and Tom belonged.   (p. 21)

Daisy lacks any meaningful integrity between self and gesture. And Gatsby, therefore, can never fully fathom her; he is too naive. His gestures and persona are too honestly an expression of the romantic self-image he has modelled himself on – despite the submerged identity of James Gatz – for him to understand Daisy's selfishness and charming duplicity.

Although Gatsby's personality may bear an honest relation to his private intentions, we must remember that the Gatsby we are discussing is largely Carraway's creation. If we sense something of Gatsby's hidden nature, an intimate knowledge Fitzgerald would deny is ever fully valid, it is because Carraway believes in the sympathetic understanding he has, at the last, for Gatsby. The sensibilities of Nick's own private character translate the public spectacle of Gatsby's personality into an apparent three-dimensionality. Nick responds to Gatsby's ludicrous poses and sentimental cliches and immense egoism with imaginative sympathy because he believes these traits are born of a romantic hopefulness that he shares.

From their first meeting, Nick translates Gatsby's gestures with authority, as if his response were singularly attuned to Gatsby's intended effect.

> He smiled understandingly – much more than understandingly. It was one of those rare smiles with a quality of eternal reassurance in it, that you may come across four or five times in life. It faced – or seemed to face – the whole external world for an instant, and then concentrated on you with an irresistible prejudice in your favor. It understood you just as far as you wanted to be understood, believed in you as you would like to believe in yourself, and assured you that it had precisely the impression of you that, at your best, you hoped to convey. Precisely at that point it vanished – and I was looking at an elegant young roughneck, a year or two over thirty, whose elaborate formality of speech just missed being absurd.   (p. 47)

Gatsby's exotic behaviour, always at the threshold between the grand and the absurd, belongs to a different tradition from the moral realism I discussed earlier in terms of Nick's growth. Dramatic flair, defiant public gesture often constitute the heart of that ideal self-image pursued by romantic heroes as they define themselves against the conventions of the community. One need think only of Manfred and Ahab, of Kurtz and Jim. Further, in Gatsby's dramatic behaviour W. J. Harvey discovers not simply a typical egoistic self-proclamation, but an articulation, even a partial, symbolic fulfilment, of Gatsby's dream.

> What we remember about [Gatsby] is not the restlessness or the drifting but 'an unbroken series of successful gestures' ... above all, Gatsby stretching out his arms towards the green light that is the vain promise of his future. We remember these formal poses as something theatrical or religious, but they *are* poses, moments of suspended time, something static and as such are the stylistic equivalents of Gatsby's attempt to impose his dream on reality, his effort to make the ever-rolling stream stand still.[12]

An essential element of Gatsby's dream, therefore, and indeed of the romantic impulse itself, is the pursuit of a transcendent significance outside of society and beyond the mutability of history. The fact that we remember Gatsby's gestures outside of the narrative flow of events is evidence of how Gatsby and Carraway are truly in league: Gatsby poses and Carraway paints the picture, capturing the instant. Initially, Nick shares his fascination with other 'moths' (p. 39) drawn to Gatsby's Trimalchean fetes. However, Gatsby's extravagance is given form and meaning only in Nick's imagination; he comes alive when Nick first glimpses the intensity of his dream. That intimation arises without Gatsby himself even present, as Jordon Baker reveals the history of his affair with Daisy.

> 'Gatsby bought that house so that Daisy would be just across the bay.'
> Then it had not been merely the stars to which he had aspired on that June night. He came alive to me, delivered suddenly from the womb of his purposeless splendor.   (p. 72)

As Harvey points out, Carraway recalls Gatsby in a series of photographic poses, each representing an aspect of Gatsby's romantic, idealized self-image. But Jordon's story reveals the key to translating the static tableaux. Not until then does Nick understand the significance of his first view of his neighbour standing in the darkness, arms stretched across the bay. The gesture acquires meaning only through the interpretation of an observer, someone whose own character provides a touchstone for understanding.[13]

Nick responds powerfully to the bare suggestion of Gatsby's dream. He is drawn to Gatsby and repelled because of the paradoxical impulses within himself as much as by the inconsistencies of the other's nature. Throughout the course of the tale Nick remains one foot in the settlement of conventional society, one foot in the wilderness with this extraordinary fellow. He is anchored to a world of chronological time and mutability, to values that are fundamentally social. Yet he is drawn imaginatively to a figure who repudiates both time and an identity defined by the community. Nick's dilemma is similar to that of narrators in such novels as *Wuthering Heights* and *The Scarlet Letter*, who straddle the traditions of realism and romanticism. They are poised between the values of the community and the creative defiance of a rebellious hero. Nick's own form of heroism, when he too becomes a narrator, will be to synthesize these apparently disparate impulses within his vision of general irony. He will avow the value of Gatsby's imagination and energy and his yearning for significance, while also affirming a code of fundamental decencies that makes human intercourse meaningful. Yet despite his allegiance to this code, Nick will have kicked himself free of the immediate social world in a way narrators before Conrad's *Heart of Darkness* never did.

IV

Nick's initial reading of Gatsby's dream senses no great mythic heroism; the fact of the dream, rather, merely suggests a meaningful pattern where before there had existed 'purposeless splendor'. Yet he seems to grasp at once that they have something in common, as if all young men have worshipped, or dreamed of worshipping an extraordinary woman. Certainly Fitzgerald's earlier fiction repeats the pattern often enough to suggest it as a universal truth.

Fitzgerald's stories also anticipate the way in which Gatsby's dream extends beyond any wordly object. Dexter Green, in 'Winter Dreams', before he focuses his desires on winning Judy Jones, is a middle-class boy with ambition and powerful, though vague yearnings.

> But do not get the impression, because his winter dreams happened to be concerned at first with musings on the rich, that there was anything merely snobbish in [Dexter]. He wanted not association with glittering things and glittering people – he wanted the glittering things themselves. Often he reached out for the best without knowing why he wanted it – and sometimes he ran up against the mysterious denials and prohibitions in which life indulges.[14]

The continuing conflict with the world's mysterious denials, dramatized in the thwarting of his desire for Judy Jones, slowly leeches the vitality of Dexter's winter dreams. These too, finally as ambiguous as Gatsby's, long for a personal significance beyond time and mutability and any merely physical object. Dexter, like Gatsby, does not easily surrender his dream, though it does fade with time. Years later, learning that Judy Jones has become a nondescript, persecuted housewife, Dexter finally capitulates to the heavy hand of the world.

He wanted to care, and he could not care. For he had gone away and he could never go back any more. The gates were closed, the sun was gone down, and there was no beauty but the gray beauty of steel that withstands all time.   (p. 75)

Dexter becomes a mature character defined by the chronological world of man that has swept away his illusions and desires. Gatsby, however, remains on the romantic frontier, forever alien to the social world even while he masters its financial mysteries; he never accepts such limitation.

Where Dexter Green learns of Judy Jones's fate at a distance, his winter dreams having ceased to be more than a memory, Gatsby pursues the fulfilment of his dreams relentlessly through the years. And the reunion of Gatsby and Daisy in Nick's cottage hints at the revelation that Daisy is the object of a dream that has transcended her.

'If it wasn't for the mist we could see your home across the bay,' said Gatsby. 'You always have a green light that burns all night at the end of your dock.'

Daisy put her arm through his abruptly, but he seemed absorbed in what he had just said. Possibly it had occurred to him that the colossal significance of that light had now vanished forever.   (p. 84)

Characteristically, Nick qualifies his interpretation with 'possibly'. The tableau is presented, Gatsby and Daisy arm in arm, he suddenly wistful and distant. The *meaning* of that tableau is drawn intuitively by Nick, and Gatsby's hidden character fleshed out in Nick's imagination that bit more.

With this scene Nick begins to recognize that the contradictions in this other man may partly be due to a dream that has longed to reach beyond the physical reality of its object. Daisy is a flawed though extraordinary creature, as Nick well knows; she can hardly live up to the conception of Gatsby's imagination. For he desires, ultimately, an object that will glorify *him*, opening before him a path to transcendent significance. Daisy is unequal to that task, being very much a creature of this world. And this further explains the paradox apparent in Gatsby; though his impulse may be romantic and lofty, his quest has led him into a fallen world. In pursuit of Daisy he has conquered society's financial mysteries, but on its own terms, and he has been stained.

The dream is also limited by the dreamer. It is not simply that Daisy, a flesh and blood 'fetish',[15] cannot live up to the enormity of Gatsby's hopes, nor that the waste land that encompasses East Egg, West Egg, and Manhattan as well as the Valley of Ashes is corrupt. The vaguely platonic dream, as Nick senses it, transcends Gatsby. It is something nobler than the egoism of his imagination and the absurd expression he gives it. The immense intensity of the dream, after all, has been shaped by the imagination of seventeen-year-old James Gatz, a conception to which Jay Gatsby remains ever faithful. Like Jim and Ashburnham, like Robert Cohn in *The Sun Also Rises,* Gatsby's romantic self-image is founded on adventure stories; his father will bring to his son's funeral the copy of *Hopalong Cassidy* in which Jimmy Gatz inscribed a schedule for his self-improvement. The categories of James Gatz's imagination can only be inadequate to shape the dream's full glory.

In creating a portrait of Gatsby and in trying to explain his own sympathy for the man, Nick Carraway must himself attempt to impose form on Gatsby's dream, to articulate its beauty and energy and value, without deadening it within the constraints of language. We can recall the similar struggle of Marlow and Dowell to impose form and meaning on tales that apparently deny all form. Both Nick's ambivalence towards Gatsby and the inevitable disjunction between the ideal and the material world are further reflected in the ways he fashions a suggestion of the dream into language. Carraway reports Gatsby's intimate confessions using three separate strategies precisely to heighten the manifold paradoxes. The first is the straightforward quotation of Gatsby's own words.

Gatsby's failure of language is another manifestation of the dream's adolescent conception. He is clumsy with language; his diction and images also belong to boyhood adventure fiction. And too, the flow of simple communication doesn't easily conform to staged poses. When he perseveres in trying to match words to gestures, he repeatedly crosses the threshold between the mysterious and the absurd.[16]

'I lived like a young rajah in all the capitals of Europe – Paris, Venice, Rome – collecting jewels, chiefly rubies, hunting big game, painting a little, things for myself only, and trying to forget something very sad that had happened to me long ago.'
With an effort I managed to restrain my incredulous laughter. The very phrases were worn so threadbare that they evoked no

image except that of a turbaned 'character' leaking sawdust at every pore as he pursued a tiger through the Bois de Boulogne.

(p. 61)

By thus reporting Gatsby's speeches verbatim and then criticizing their heavy-handed cliches, Nick stakes out one dimension in Gatsby – with these brief glimpses the full, exotic, impossibility of such a creature becomes apparent. Indeed, the extravagance of this passage distances the reader so that he is taken aback by Nick's abrupt conversion moments later on seeing Gatsby's medal from Montenegro: 'Then it was all true' (p. 62).

Yet absurdity is, of course, only one element of Nick's portrait of Gatsby. A second method is simple paraphrasis; Nick translates the gist of Gatsby's speech without being bound by the artificial constrictions of the other's syntax and diction.

He talked a lot about the past, and I gathered that he wanted to recover something, some idea of himself perhaps, that had gone into loving Daisy. His life had been confused and disordered since then, but if he could once return to a certain starting place and go over it all slowly, he could find out what that thing was. ...

(p. 99, Fitzgerald's ellipsis)

Nick's paraphrasing here keeps absurdity at a distance. Gatsby is *not* entirely unaware of the tyranny of change. The intensity of his first great love has shorn him of something of himself, some essence of vitality that nurtured his belief in romantic possibility. This narrative strategy conveys both the strength and pathos of Gatsby's yearning, along with Nick's own ironic awareness that, as he has said to Gatsby moments before, 'You can't repeat the past'.

Immediately after this last passage, Carraway abandons Gatsby's words entirely. He transforms into lyric the story of Gatsby in Louisville five years earlier.

Now it was a cool night with that mysterious excitement in it which comes at the two changes of the year. The quiet lights in the houses were humming out into the darkness and there was a stir and bustle among the stars. Out of the corner of his eye Gatsby saw that the blocks of the sidewalks really formed a ladder and mounted to a secret place above the tree – he could climb to it, if he climbed alone, and once there he could suck on the pap of life, gulp down the incomparable milk of wonder.   (pp. 99–100)

Clearly this is more than a matter of substituting new words for Gatsby's – the perspective, the conception, as well as the language, are Nick's. He has, in fact, stolen away dream from dreamer, and reshaped it according to the possibilities of his own imagination. Here, when Gatsby's dream seems most vivid, we discover to what extent both Gatsby and his dream are Nick's creations. He can speak as Gatsby cannot, achieving lyric intensity rather than empty cliche, for as narrator he possesses at once an ironic detachment from and a sympathetic bond to Gatsby's romantic impulse.

But finally what Nick cannot say – and does not attempt – is the most potent testament that the two men share a dream that transcends either of them. Nick, like Gatsby, cannot circumscribe its energy, the vitality of all youth and hope and desire, within the boundaries of language. Instead, with Conradian impressionism, he *suggests* the dream's deeper significance.

> Through all he said, even through his appalling sentimentality, I was reminded of something – an elusive rhythm, a fragment of lost words, that I had heard somewhere a long time ago. For a moment a phrase tried to take shape in my mouth and my lips parted like a dumb man's, as though there was more struggling upon them than a wisp of startled air. But they made no sound, and what I had almost remembered was uncommunicable forever.   (p. 100)

Nick acknowledges the greatness of the dream by not constraining it, not fashioning it fully into articulateness. Yet by evoking the dream through language, he achieves what Gatsby cannot – he translates the ideal into a medium of this world, affirming its value, and sustaining it.

V

Just as the ideal cannot be brought into the physical universe without being tainted, Gatsby cannot survive in a world indifferent to his dream and unable to comprehend him. With Daisy, the object that has sustained his dream and given his life direction, lost forever, Gatsby's personality collapses. It will be Nick as narrator and hero who revives the dream and sets it in juxtaposition to a modern society always its foe.

Certainly Gatsby generates and bears his own fate; he has no place in a world that grants him everything but what he desires most, the right it cannot grant – to change time and history. Like a great carnival with tents struck and costumes shed, he ceases entirely to exist as far as society is concerned. Only Nick, acting according to the moral gyroscope of his identity, that code of fundamental decencies, insists on Gatsby's significance, his meaning as a human being, if not the transcendent significance Jimmy Gatz had dreamed of.

> [A]s he lay in his house and didn't move or breathe or speak, hour upon hour, it grew upon me that I was responsible, because no one else was interested – interested, I mean, with that intense personal interest to which every one has some vague right at the end. (p. 145)

The refusal of all the crowd who had swirled through Gatsby's parties to recognize such human responsibilities is finally more damning in Nick's eyes than any collective guilt for Gatsby's fate. All that holds this society together – and not just Tom and Daisy as representative of the very rich – is a vast, careless, self-interested association. No code of solidarity to the social weal, or moral responsibility, or human dignity, retains any forceful imperative.

The indifference of society itself to standards of human behaviour destroys Nick's faith in what Marlow called 'a sovereign code of conduct'. Carraway must henceforth wrestle with the fact that any such code is arbitrary, artificial, and, to a certain degree, an illusion. Right action, which in the innocence of youth had seemed automatic and unquestionable, becomes a matter of deliberate choice. Carraway's choice to assume responsibility for Gatsby is a response to the indifferent, to Meyer Wolfsheim and to Daisy, to the East and to the universe – a clear, unabashed claim of his own moral identity.

Of course, Gatsby has been no more committed than other members of Eastern society to a common code of shared values. While eagerly pursuing his own glory he could hardly be distracted with moral imperatives. Gatsby's physical existence, his methods of surviving and conquering, all the tools he has used in his quest, are as corrupt as any of the creatures around him.

Carraway's rejection of the East for its irresponsibility, therefore, is a rejection as well of that side of Gatsby's nature which, like Kurtz's, asserts the appetite and significance of the ego in disregard of larger forms of human relations. His enduring ambivalence towards Gatsby is not due solely to the conflict between the dream and the corrupt environment in which it is expressed, but to this essential aspect of the romantic impulse as well – that it celebrates the self alone, not the values that make community meaningful.

Earlier I argued that the underlying motive of Gatsby's dream is an urge towards personal transcendent significance: a defiant I am, or better, *I mean*, hurled out into a universe of turmoil and indifference. Even as he repudiates its anti-social nature, Nick, as narrator, affirms Gatsby's dream with his own effort to create a meaningful tale that will endure. Gatsby sought to set himself free of worldly, temporal constraints. Nick's heroism is to succeed, at least partly, where Gatsby fails. The victory of the narrative itself is analogous to and greater than Gatsby's characteristic gestures or poses. W. J. Harvey suggested that those static poses were a 'stylistic equivalent' to Gatsby's goal, an existence momentarily free of time. Nick's narrative is a more enduring stylistic equivalent of what the dream promised – an existence outside of time, immutable, brought to life in the eyes of an audience.

The narrative is also the culmination of what Nick has begun by accepting responsibility for Gatsby. By telling the tale Nick assumes a further responsibility: for the dream itself. His narrative circumscribes its romantic egoism, while celebrating its vitality and faith, its capacity for wonder, and its determination to create significance. And the narrative fulfils that determination. It insists on the form – and the meaning – of a tale that has apparently ended in disaster and chaos. Out of the confusion following Gatsby's death, and the hypocrisy and indifference of New York society, emerges Nick Carraway's moral character, manifested in the controlling irony that shapes the tale and answers the chaos.

In nineteenth-century novels of moral education, proof of the hero's new character is borne out by his willing integration into the social fabric of time and labour and responsibility. Nick Carraway's new identity, however, involves something other than a synthesis of his private values and desires with the external realities of the social environment; his modern form of heroism synthesizes the essential impulses of nineteenth-century heroes of realism with the romantic heroism of a Gatsby. For his actions after Gatsby's death are directed by a pervading recognition of general irony which steadfastly holds true to a social code of human responsibilities, affirms the romantic urge towards individual significance, and yet recognizes as well the radical relativism of all values and dreams.

Rather than plunging once more into the turmoil of life in New York, Nick repudiates it, retreating West. Yet to what precisely he has returned remains an enigma. Like Marlow and Dowell, Carraway as he speaks seems isolated from the immediate flux of life by the distance of his own narrative frame, reflecting the ironic detachment of his soul. He too has been partly lamed by his acquired sensibility. What had been a characteristic stance of being 'within and without' has become, we sense, more radical. Nick at the conclusion seems singularly 'without'. When he speaks of the Mid-West it is not of the present in which he finds himself, but of the past, a memory that exists outside of time much as does the story he tells.

> That's my Middle West – not the wheat or the prairies of the lost Swede towns, but the thrilling returning trains of my youth, and the street lamps and sleigh bells in the frosty dark and the shadows of holly wreaths thrown by lighted windows on the snow. I am part of that, a little solemn with the feel of those long winters, a little complacent from growing up in the Carraway house in a city where dwellings are still called through decades by a family's name. (p. 155)

Having reconsecrated those human values passed on to him by his father, Nick seeks to return to a traditional society in which they remain the unconscious sinews of community. He pursues a quest similar to Gatsby's after all – a journey back towards an innocence and security now lost, towards something of himself that has vanished. His West is a memory of childhood. Carraway, again like Gatsby, wishes that all that has happened, not just this past summer but since the War, can be redeemed with an act of will and spirit. At the same time, however, he is well aware that such a wish is folly. The heroic urge for transcendent significance remains potent – impels him to speak – even as he is 'borne back ceaselessly into the past' (p. 159).

Carraway has been changed as Marlow was changed. How comfortably a spiritual orientation of general irony can meld into the work-a-day reality of the West remains an open question. Nick gives us no suggestion of what his new life has brought – as if he, though not the rest of the world, has remained 'at a sort of moral attention' until the tale is told.

5

The Sun Also Rises:
Heroism of Innocence,
Heroism of a Fallen World

I

You ought to be ironical the minute you get out of bed.[1]

Ernest Hemingway read *The Great Gatsby* with admiration shortly after meeting Scott Fitzgerald in the spring of 1925. By the summer of that year, after a disastrous return to the fiesta in Pamplona, he had begun work on a novel that, whatever its characteristics as a *roman-à-clef*, bore a striking resemblance to *Gatsby*. Hemingway had already worked with Ford Madox Ford on *The Transatlantic Review*. In a special supplement to that quarterly on the death of Joseph Conrad he had printed the famous tribute that, could he bring Conrad back to life 'by grinding Mr. Eliot into a fine, dry powder and sprinkling that powder over Conrad's grave', he would 'leave for London … with a sausage grinder'.[2] The spiritual as well as structural kinship between *The Sun Also Rises* and *Heart of Darkness*, *Lord Jim*, and *The Good Soldier*, is hardly accidental. Yet when Hemingway refashions the familiar pattern to suit his own design, he transforms it as well. As with our other narrators, Jake Barnes is lame and passive. Yet his disillusionment with traditional social values is not a discovery made during the tale: it is the ground for that tale, shared with a generation wounded by the war and alienated from the past. And the heir to such romantic figures as Jim and Gatsby is a wretched fellow named Cohn, dismissed from the novel before its conclusion. His place is taken by Pedro Romero, whose heroic roots lie in a different tradition from the particular romanticism of the nineteenth-century novel. From the start, therefore, the *givens* of this story are markedly different from the others, and with Romero's assumption of Cohn's role arrives the end of the pattern initiated by Conrad. In the same tradition as

92

Marlow, Dowell, and Carraway, however, Jake Barnes emerges as the true hero of *The Sun Also Rises*, a hero appropriate to a modern world of lapsed values and fragmented rituals.

Early on in *The Sun Also Rises* Brett Ashley squeezes away from Jake into one corner of a cab as they ride through the Paris evening, she afraid of being aroused by a man who, though she claims to love him, cannot physically satisfy her. And the story closes in Madrid, Jake and Brett once more in a cab, she clinging to him this time, he apparently little moved and sharply sarcastic. Jake's journey from one cab to the other – that is the tale.

The central question it raises is whether that journey has in fact brought Jake anywhere, whether he has learned, grown, been significantly changed by the experience, or simply been carried back to begin the cycle anew. Although critics have likened the novel to a prose *Waste Land* and argued that Jake remains unchanged, as impotent as the Fisher-King,[3] he has, as we shall see, in fact accomplished a significant spiritual journey from that initial infernal taxi ride with Brett. It is suggestive to note that in recent years a gradual reappraisal has found *The Waste Land* itself – which Hemingway, despite his avowed preference for Conrad, had read and admired – not so irreparably bleak. The Fisher-King too, wounded, tentative, and weak, has nevertheless journeyed to the shore. He sits fishing, gathering fragments of a shattered culture about him and creating new form – that of the poem. The heroic task of Jake's narrative will be much the same.

In Spain, Jake has betrayed himself and his private values of honour and *aficion*. By accepting responsibility for that failure, he will be able to affirm the same values publicly, setting them in juxtaposition to a darker recognition of social hypocrisy and of an indifferent universe. General irony is once more the fruit of a moral education, the foundation for new character, and the structural principle of a narrative. And again the public telling of the tale will represent a culminating heroic gesture, ratifying all that Jake has become, while generating new form for the fragmented images of modern experience.

The interplay between the novel's epigraphs reveals from the start the governing sensibility of Jake's narrative: of a man's unending struggle against both the maiming pressures of human history and the vast indifferent sweep of the natural world. Despite a tendency on the part of critics to pick one epigraph or the other as a touchstone to the novel,[4] they may better be seen as paired or juxtaposed.

You are all a lost generation.

One generation passeth away, and another generation cometh; but the earth abideth forever ... The sun also riseth, and the sun also goeth down, and hasteth to the place where he arose ... The wind goeth toward the south, and turneth about into the north; it whirleth about continually, and the wind returneth again according to his circuits ... All the rivers run into the sea; yet the sea is not full; unto the place from whence the rivers come, thither they return again.

The notion of a lost generation resonates beyond those who have survived the Great War. *Any* generation, any individual will be lost in the sweep of time, as Ecclesiastes affirms. The first epigraph focuses on the single generation alienated by its own history; the second on the cycles and seasons of the earth which impassively engulf all generations.

Two closely related questions, then, are immediately posed for the novel: what, if anything, that man achieves can endure, and how may he, faced with what the older waiter in 'A Clean, Well-Lighted Place' calls *nada* – imminent darkness and nullity – create even limited meaning for his life. In Hemingway's fiction these questions arise again and again, always with the certainty that whatever you did 'they killed you in the end'.[5] Nevertheless, Hemingway's heroes establish harbours of light by steadfastly facing the *nada* with courage and integrity, by remaining faithful to human codes, and, for brief moments, by loving. In *The Sun Also Rises*, that second taxi ride with Brett represents Jake's courageous acceptance of his own responsibility in the face of meaninglessness and betrayal. And the tale he goes on to tell may be 'so humanly true that it will outlast the vagaries of time and change'.[6] To create something timeless that yet affirms those values threatened always by time: that surely is heroic achievement.

II

Jake Barnes in Paris, taking that first cab with Brett Ashley, is already thoroughly disillusioned. Marlow may be worldly wise, Nick Carraway restless and possessing an in-born sense of irony, but each retains a certain initial innocence. Through their relationships with Kurtz and Gatsby, they slowly discover the corruption of modern society and the arbitrariness of its standards. This perception they wed to a stubborn faith in the value of more traditional, communal codes and the possibilities of the human imagination. Jake, however, has long since lost touch with any such faith. Nor can he retreat towards the past. Paris is home, his daily round a patterned series of empty rituals for keeping isolation, loneliness, and meaninglessness at bay.

The history of change in Jake begins, then, well before the opening of *The Sun Also Rises*. As many critics have noted, the Nick Adams stories are a prelude to Jake's character. From young boy to father, Nick Adams passes through stages of growth and loss of innocence. Stories such as 'Now I Lay Me' and 'A Way You'll Never Be' directly anticipate Jake's present afflictions, wounded in the war, unable to sleep at night, haunted with fears. By placing Jake Barnes in the context of Hemingway's larger body of fiction we thus locate him – though this a partial truth – as one of the 'Nick Adams-heroes' or what Earl Rovit calls a *tyro*: a character alert and sensitive, often wounded in some way by his exaggerated sensitivity.[7]

This context also heightens what can in any event be gleaned from hints in the story: Jake Barnes was once active, having chosen to fly on the Italian front. He not only possessed culturally-inspired ideals that led him to war; he was something of a conventional hero. For his efforts, however, he was wounded and disillusioned, having changed nothing. Like Nick Adams in 'A Very Short Story' and Frederic Henry in *A Farewell to Arms*, and Hemingway himself, when wounded Jake falls in love – with all the passion of a first great love – with one of the women nursing him, Brett Ashley.

But at this point Jake's similarities with Hemingway's other heroes end abruptly. Though deeply marked physically and emotionally, Adams and Henry recover from their wounds. Jake has been more deeply maimed, spiritually as well as physically. And Brett is no Catherine Barkley, eager to cut her hair to look like Henry. She has lost her 'true love' (p. 39) in the war and married a mad

Baronet who has abused her; for all her avowals of love for Jake, she has been wounded as deeply as he and is no more able to consummate, spiritually at least, a meaningful relationship.

Jake Barnes is, in a very real sense, an objective correlative to the spiritual bankruptcy of the colony of expatriates in Paris. All the Paris crowd seems wounded. Mike Campbell and Count Mippipopolous each bear scars. As Georgette, the *poule* Jake picks up in boredom and self-mockery, remarks when he pushes her hand away, 'Everybody's sick. I'm sick too' (p. 15). That Jake's wound is more severe than the others' is due not only to the chance of war; as the most sensitive member of the community, he has been struck most deeply by the great disillusionment with a society that has lost its innocence and many of its shared values. His hurt is the physical representation of other characters' less visible disorders. The essential characteristic of Jake's life in Paris owes as much to Tiresias, observant, sensitive, and passive, as to the Fisher-King.

Alone among the characters of the novel, however, Jake *does* work. He puts in his hours each day, attending interviews, gathering gossip, dispatching dispatches, dodging Cohn's interruptions, explaining to Brett that he cannot carouse all night, and conscientiously ensuring that his office will be in order during his holiday. His work matters; it reinforces the integrity of his character. Despite the fact that 'in the newspaper business ... it is such an important part of the ethics that you should never seem to be working' (p. 11), Jake draws a sustenance, a sense of responsibility, similar to the sanity-saving duties of Marlow's labour in *Heart of Darkness*. Yet the few hours a day of routine drill hardly carry the moral heft that labour possesses for Conrad. Nor do they significantly counter-balance the empty rituals of Jake's general regimen.

Although much of his daily round is intended to dull his awareness of *nada* and isolation, Jake does not lack a personal 'philosophy' – a means of justifying the life he lives. In this system no transcendent principles reside. What values (or pleasures) are found must be paid for. Rightly appreciating the cost of how one chooses to live, what pleasure one takes – even the pleasure of ironic disengagement – depends on having lived long enough or intensely enough or having been wounded so as to be disillusioned with traditional registers of worth. One must see things for what they 'are'. Jake's eventual repudiation of this code will be an important gauge in assessing his change in character.

This code of value-exchange is not Jake's alone, of course; in one form or another, the other members of the Paris clan practise it. Count Mippipopulous is its corpulent genius. He too has been wounded: the arrow scars he dramatically displays are physical evidence. As Brett several times insists, he is 'one of us'. The Count has long ago learned the sources from which he can draw most pleasure. He loves cigars, fine brandy and champagne, and is 'always in love' (p. 62). 'That is the secret. You must get to know the values', he confides to Jake. Nevertheless, Mippipopolous is something of a grotesque, making use of Brett every bit as much as she uses him, speaking English either as ridiculously formal as Gatsby's or as corrupt as Wolfsheim's. 'You don't need a title. You got class all over you', he assures Brett (p. 59).

When Jake later articulates his own version of the code, shortly before the climax of the fiesta in Pamplona, his tone is not so smugly complacent as the Count's. It reveals two important attitudes: that the 'philosophy' has been for him a means for imposing a simplifying pattern on the infinitely complex and fluid life that has already wounded him – a means for keeping that life safely at arm's length – and, secondly, that he has already begun to recognize how distorting a pattern it is.

I thought I had paid for everything. Not like the woman pays and pays and pays. No idea of retribution or punishment. Just exchange of values. You gave up something and got something else. Or you worked for something. You paid some way for everything that was any good. I paid my way into enough things that I liked, so that I had a good time. Either you paid by learning about them, or by experience, or by taking chances, or by money. Enjoying living was learning to get your money's worth and knowing when you had it. You could get your money's worth. The world was a good place to buy in. It seemed like a fine philosophy. In five years, I thought, it will seem just as silly as all the other fine philosophies I've had.   (p. 148)

What follows is more important still, a step beyond this recapitulation of the past. For Jake stands on a threshold. What his life has been since the war, and the detached, nearly impersonal safety of a code founded on barter, seems suddenly inadequate. It has neither sufficiently protected him from life nor allowed him to live. Thoroughly dissatisfied, and as yet uncertain of what sort of change is possible or where it might lead, he suspects that one can, after all, learn from life, uncovering enduring truths in the very struggle to survive and to understand.

> Perhaps as you went along you did learn something. I did not care what it was all about. All I wanted to know was how to live in it. Maybe if you found out how to live in it you learned from that what it was all about.

III

Not Brett and not the bull-fights of Pamplona, but the relationship of Jake Barnes and Robert Cohn, their profound similarities and differences, is the dynamic focus for much of *The Sun Also Rises*. Once again, a narrator's education is bound to another character, romantic and innocent, egoistic and absurd, in whose defeat Jake will spy some essential hopefulness on which to found his own new identity.

Robert Cohn has also been wounded, not by the war but in a college gym. His flattened nose is a correlative to Jake's malady, a physical testament to his role as Jake's double. Yet his posture is aggressive rather than passive, his wound hardly more than cosmetic, a mark of the ridiculous. Cohn is *not* 'one of us' in the same sense as Count Mippipopolous. He is an outsider partly because of his race, more because his innocence remains unassailably intact. We may recall Lord Jim's imperturbable innocence in face of disaster. But Jim was 'one of us' – Cohn is not.

Marlow's audience, the group whose sensibilities he shared before his experiences with Kurtz and Jim, was made up of men who shared code and tradition, and who drew strength from cultural roots in England. The social illusions that supported their identities remained intact until Marlow told his tale. Jake's crowd in Paris is far different. Their illusions have long since been shattered by the Great War. Brett's England has squandered nearly a full generation of its young men, and Jake seems irretrievably cut off from any Oak Park, Illinois. Where the foundations of Marlow's character are shaken as he recognizes that Jim's failure aboard the *Patna* signals that any 'sovereign code of conduct' is a fiction, in Jake Barnes's Paris all the crowd has suffered comparable disillusionment. Jim was 'one of us' because, on the surface at least, his innocence survived. But in the quarter-century between *Lord Jim* and *The Sun Also Rises* the world has changed. Robert Cohn is an outsider precisely because so many of his own dreams endure.

If the relationship of Jake and Cohn lies at the heart of the novel, the clash of illusions born of Cohn's romantic egoism with Jake's self-effacing care to make it from day to day is the catalyst to the central story. Cohn has been reading W. H. Hudson's *The Purple Land*. As with Jim, Ashburnham, and Gatsby, such a fable gaudily sketches an ideal self-image that the naive romantic soul will pursue relentlessly. Cohn, Jake testifies, takes the prescription of *The Purple Land* 'as literally as though it had been an R. G. Dun report' (p. 9). At thirty-four Cohn suddenly believes he has neither sufficiently lived nor explored available possibilities for adventure. How different this sensibility is from the code of exchange practised by Count Mippipopolous and Jake, which depends precisely on having *lived* so that illusion has been purged. Pleading with Jake to accompany him in search of adventure, Cohn insists they must make the most of life.

> 'Listen, Jake,' he leaned forward on the bar. 'Don't you ever get the feeling that all your life is going by and you're not taking advantage of it? Do you realize you've lived nearly half the time you have to live already?'
> 'Yes, every once in a while.'
> 'Do you know that in about thirty-five years more we'll be dead?'
> 'What the hell, Robert,' I said. 'What the hell.' (p. 11)

Jake misinterprets his eagerness, assuming that Cohn, like himself, is seeking to escape self-consciousness by 'moving from one place to another'. Cohn, however, desires not to lose but to discover his true heroic nature according to romantic formulae. Travel seems, momentarily, the thing. But adventurous journeys are only one route to romantic glory – a great love is the other. And Jake has already given us the clue: 'I am sure he had never been in love in his life' (p. 8). That same evening in a *bal musette* Cohn watches Brett Ashley, looking 'as his compatriot must have looked when he saw the promised land. Cohn, of course, was much younger. But he had that look of eager, deserving expectation' (p. 22).

The mock-heroic simile linking Robert Cohn and Moses under-scores one simple fact: for all his dreams of heroic grandeur, Cohn is inescapably absurd. Whatever bond Jake may feel to Cohn, whatever their similarities, Jake feels that this reflects only discredit on himself.

All that was ridiculous in Jim and Gatsby is intensified with Cohn. Nothing finally redeems him – no intensity of spirit or heroic longing or triumphant imagination. He lacks the single-mindedness to dominate his fate and the immediate social world even for a brief moment. It may well be that no such thing is possible in Paris. But failure accentuates his weakness, his illusion, and his absurdity.

Perspective is an important factor in this portrait, of course, and Jake, whatever sympathy he may feel, will never testify that Cohn 'is worth the whole damn bunch put together'. Jake's deep ambivalence marks the opening pages of the narrative frame with a curious tone: a mixture rather harsh, even snide, and with ill-concealed traces of envy. This is hardly the attitude of wise elevation we expect from a narrator who is also, if my claim be true, the novel's hero.

> I mistrust all frank and simple people, especially when their stories hold together, and I always had a suspicion that perhaps Robert Cohn had never been middleweight boxing champion, and that perhaps a horse had stepped on his face, or that maybe his mother had been frightened or seen something, or that he had, maybe, bumped into something as a young child, but I finally had somebody verify the story.   (p. 4)

Jake has already announced that he isn't 'much impressed' by Cohn's boxing prowess. But the issue must have significance – it opens the narrative, though it seems to have little direct relevance to Book One. Yet early on, Cohn's willingness to confront the world actively, in the ring if nowhere else, contrasts with Jake's own passivity.

More important to understanding the latent bitterness of the opening frame, however, especially since I contend that Jake has been deeply changed, is the fact that Cohn's fists have figured so dramatically in the crisis. Jake has been pummelled by them during the climactic moments of the story he is about to tell. Robert Cohn's striking out has finally, ironically, chased him from the scene; as he knocks Pedro Romero to the ground time and time again it is Romero who triumphs by continuing to rise. Yet Cohn has already beaten Jake Barnes senseless, stripped from him a habit of self-deception, and forced him to face a new and terrifying world. Raw self-awareness remains tender as Jake begins the story, therefore, and Robert Cohn takes rather a beating in his turn.

Cohn's heroic impulses and romantic imagination are also undercut by internal inconsistency; he is self-conscious and emotionally weak; he is too 'nice'. Such women as Frances Clyne, who deceive and manipulate by pretending affection, have preyed on this vulnerability.

No one had ever made him feel he was a Jew, and hence any different than anyone else, until he went to Princeton. He was a nice boy, a friendly boy, and very shy, and it made him bitter. He took it out in boxing, and he came out of Princeton with painful self-consciousness and the flattened nose, and was married by the first girl who was nice to him.   (p. 4)

Throughout *The Sun Also Rises* Cohn repeatedly stands up from tables as if to fight those who have offended him, but he is nevertheless abused mercilessly by Frances Clyne, Bill Gorton, and Mike Campbell, and impotent to stop it.

If Jake mocks Cohn's vulnerability to the machinations of women, it is partly because he too is self-conscious, though not so blindly. Brett Ashley has been no less manipulative than Frances Clyne, merely less dissembling. Jake protects himself as Cohn does not, keeping the company of men or of prostitutes who can demand of him nothing. But Brett can still reduce him to tears of frustration and to the same sort of pleading – 'Couldn't we live together, Brett? Couldn't we just live together?' (p. 56) – that makes Cohn publicly ridiculous. In lashing out at Cohn, Jake not accidently strikes himself as well. The harsh tone of the opening is ameliorated somewhat when Jake admits that he has 'not shown Robert Cohn clearly' and that 'until he fell in love with Brett, I never heard him make one remark that would, in any way, detach him from other people' (p. 45). This man, Jake's double, has loved the same woman and has been castrated by her. Here we find the other motive for Jake's bitterness; though only briefly, Cohn was able to satisfy Brett Ashley physically as Jake could not. Brett suggests the comparison herself – heedlessly – when she refuses to let Jake go with her to San Sebastian because it is 'better' for them both, then secretly departs with Cohn the next day.

IV

During the fishing trip to Burguete, a dramatic interlude, Jake demonstrates what was not readily apparent earlier – a sensitivity to the natural world and, more important, to the virtues of man's proper orientation towards it. Jake and Bill Gorton purify themselves for what is to come and are renewed by the rituals of fishing and the simple clarity of male community. As hero and narrator, Jake will later translate the values he practises in Burguete into a code with which to confront the bleak formlessness of life in Paris.

The spiritual sensitivity that is Jake's most telling characteristic throughout the rest of the novel transforms the countryside and the peasants; it transforms every action of the day, from drinking wine to cleaning fish, into something meaningful if done *properly*. Jake and Bill possess that sensitivity; Robert Cohn does not.

> After a while we came out of the mountains, and there were trees along both sides of the road, and a stream and ripe fields of grain, and the road went on, very white and straight ahead, and then lifted to a little rise, and off on the left was a hill with an old castle, with buildings close around it and a field of grain going right up to the walls and shifting in the wind. I was up in front with the driver and I turned around. Robert Cohn was asleep, but Bill looked and nodded his head.   (p. 93)

No single detail of the fishing trip is charged with exceptional meaning; the aggregate of actions and the on-going process that binds them together are what matter. Jake addresses himself to fishing with the same care a priest brings to the consecration of the host. As in 'Big, Two-Hearted River', such piety of attention creates the resonance of ritual, and through their labours Nick Adams and Jake Barnes are cleansed and renewed.

> I laid [the trout] out, side by side, all their heads pointing the same way, and I looked at them. They were beautifully colored and firm and hard from the cold water. It was a hot day, so I slit them all and shucked out the insides, gills and all, and tossed them over across the river. I took the trout ashore, washed them in the cold, smoothly heavy water above the dam, and then picked some ferns and packed them all in the bag, three trout on

a layer of ferns, then another layer of ferns, then three more trout, and then covered them with ferns.   (pp. 119–20)

The activity is sanctified by its simplicity and by a deeper significance we sense penetrating it. That hidden dimension is communicated through Jake's art as narrator; if he is to some extent a priest of man's relations with the wilderness, his task extends beyond the moment of fishing to the successful translation of spirit into prose. In striking contrast to the rest of the novel, irony has little role in this passage. Jake wants not to detach the reader from the experience, but to make it seem both ultimate and immediate. Only later, as he attempts to carry some of the same spiritual values into his new role in the social world, does general irony become a necessity. It will juxtapose these values to a radically sceptical attitude towards modern life, and scenes such as this in Burguete to the dreary world of Paris.

Jake's sensitivity to ritual, in Burguete and elsewhere, reveals a paradox within his own wounded soul: that he can be so attuned to man's deepest needs and yet follow a pattern of life-denying customs in Paris to deaden those needs. The paradox is played out in Burguete, ritual reappearing even while parodied in a scene of thanksgiving.

> 'Utilize a little, brother,' he handed me the bottle. 'Let us not doubt, brother. Let us not pry into the holy mysteries of the hen-coop with simian fingers. Let us accept on faith and simply say – I want you to join with me in saying – what shall we say, brother?' He pointed the drumstick at me and went on. 'Let me tell you. We will say, and I for one am proud to say – and I want you to say with me, on your knees, brother. Let no man be ashamed to kneel here in the great out-of-doors. Remember the woods were God's first temples. Let us kneel and say: "Don't eat that, Lady – that's Mencken."'   (p. 122)

Bill's irreverent tone doesn't undercut the moment's significance –all kidding aside, both men are genuinely thankful. To pray explicitly, all kidding aside, however, might endanger their immediate exhilaration. Traditional prayers have become empty forms without potency, recalled only in bastardized parody.

The rituals of Burguete are juxtaposed not only to those of Paris and Pamplona but, as in the thanksgiving, to the Church which is present in all three. Only Jake remains receptive, if distantly, to the Church and to the values it represents. When the men visit the monastery of Roncesvalle, Bill and their new friend Harris are uncomfortable; they've come only out of some distant sense of obligation. They are as out of place as Brett will be in the churches of Pamplona.

> 'It's a remarkable place, though,' Harris said. 'I wouldn't not have seen it. I'd been intending coming up each day.'
> 'It isn't the same as fishing, though, is it?' Bill asked.   (p. 128)

Jake has remained silent. The Church retains some distantly remembered significance for him. He reveals towards it the same sensitivity that he has for fishing and that will mark him as one of the elect *aficionados* in Pamplona. He goes to church; he confesses; he prays. And though the prayers often lead nowhere, he maintains a faint but essential hopefulness that in the future he will be a 'better' Catholic. This spiritual openness – and yearning – which we first see in Burguete defines his character as profoundly as does his wound, and makes credible his later moral transformation.

> I was a little ashamed, and regretted that I was such a rotten Catholic, but realized there was nothing I could do about it, at least for a while, and maybe never, but that anyway it was a grand religion, and I only wished I felt religious and maybe I would the next time.   (p. 97)

Like Bill and Harris, like Brett, Jake gets little immediate nurture from the Church, certainly less than from fishing or bull-fights; but he *hopes* as the others cannot. That hope, finally, will be the mortar bonding the central paradox of general irony. For only with an essential hopefulness can courage and art and community resist the chaos of the darker side of the world's contradictions.

V

In the wilderness and among men, Jake demonstrates honesty and spiritual vitality, but his relations with the larger social world are far different. During the fiesta in Pamplona, a 'nightmare' (p. 222), he so thoroughly betrays himself that he must at last acknowledge his passive, self-deceiving character for what it is. The pain, the nakedness, and the humiliation of that experience lay open the possibility of discovering a new foundation for moral character and, ultimately, for heroic responsibility.

The borders of the settlement, which usually keep out the threatening chaos of the uncivilized while burying human primal passions deeply within, are deliberately broken down during the fiesta. The ritual-art of the bullfighter seizes the chaos, subdues it to form and meaningfulness, and re-establishes human boundaries. As narrator, Jake will perform a similar task, imposing narrative order and the moral perspective of general irony on the apparent chaos of events.

One of the first casualties of the fiesta is the certainty of everyday values.

> The peasants were in the outlying wine-shops. There they were drinking, getting ready for the fiesta. They had come in so recently from the plains and the hills that it was necessary that they make their shifting in values gradually. They could not start in paying cafe prices. They got their money's worth in the wine-shops. Money still had a definite value in hours worked and bushels of grain sold. Late in the fiesta it would not matter what they paid, nor where they bought. (p. 152)

Value and payment lose all meaning. And the philosophy by which Jake has shielded himself and regulated his life in Paris becomes an empty jumble of words. Yet although it threatens his customary detachment, Jake annually seeks out this maelstrom. Fishing in Burguete has not satisfied his thirst for spiritual renewal. In Pamplona, sources that were distinct or contradictory elsewhere meet at the same well-spring. The Church is not a peripheral anachronism as in Paris or set in contrast to the natural world as in Burguete; it *authorizes* the fiesta so that, as pagan energy swirls, diminishing the Christian procession but never quite overwhelming it, Church and peasants together can draw on deep springs of spirit and passion. The wild frenzy of the *riau-riau* dancers surrounds the 'translation' (pp. 154–5) of San Fermin from church to church, fever swelling towards release in the heart of the fiesta, the bull-fight.

Jake's sensibility draws him as well to the passion, the *aficion*, of the bull-fight. Those who share *aficion* form a community within the festival's general mob. An invisible talisman of understanding cuts across superficial distinctions of heritage and language. Although Montoya's friends may be sceptical, when Jake has satisfied their oblique questioning they draw him into the brotherhood with a laying-on of hands.

> When they saw that I had aficion, and there was no password, no set questions that could bring it out, rather it was a sort of oral spiritual examination with the questions always a little on the defensive and never apparent, there was this same embarrassed putting the hand on the shoulder, or a 'Buen Hombre.' But nearly always there was the actual touching. It seemed as though they wanted to touch you to make it certain.   (p. 132)

For all its shared spiritual engagement, however, *aficion* belongs to observers outside the ring. They experience the 'disturbed emotional feeling that always comes after a bull-fight, and the feeling of elation that comes after a good bull-fight' (p. 164), but they do not actively participate. They, Jake among them, must remain passive. Even within the passion of the festival, Jake's character remains as tame as in Paris. He protects himself, unwilling to risk being wounded again.

Among the group who have come with him to Pamplona, Jake's passivity extends still further, becoming an unspoken identification with steers in the ring. He is led about and gored at the whim of others' passions.

> 'They let the bulls out of the cages one at a time, and they have steers in the corral to receive them and keep them from fighting, and the bulls tear in at the steers and the steers run around like old maids trying to quiet them down.'   (p. 133)

In Pamplona, Robert Cohn is every bit as much a steer as Jake. Although aggressive in Paris in a way Jake could not be, and briefly triumphant in San Sebastian, Robert Cohn has been emotionally castrated by Brett. He is reduced and lampooned far beyond anything that happened to Jim, Ashburnham, or Gatsby. Cohn's great love has been a La Dolciquita, selfish, hard, and shallow, taking as much of his spiritual vitality as was to be got and then discarding him, rather than a Nancy Rufford, a woman willing to adore and nurture his own ideal self-image. And at this stage

Hemingway begins to move beyond the pattern of those earlier novels. The romantic figure disappears, having been humiliated, his place assumed by another sort of hero, Pedro Romero, who will serve as tutor and exemplar to Jake.

While he remains at the festival, however, romantic egoism continues to be Cohn's driving impulse. He can neither imagine nor accept that something vitally important to his self-image can lack transcendent value; he flounders deeper and deeper into absurdity, wishing desperately that Brett will acknowledge that the brief affair in San Sebastian *meant* something. But no enduring meaning is possible: for he has refused ever to see Brett for what she is – early on he insisted to Jake that she was 'something fine and straight' (p. 38) – preferring instead to fashion her according to the demands of his dream. And he has sought ratification of that dream in the eyes of others.

Pedro Romero, who will take Cohn's place in Brett Ashley's bed and as the central heroic figure of the fiesta, demonstrates *his* love for Brett by exercising his art for himself and, through the strength and certainty he taps within, only then for her. The eyes of all the world are on him, but he does not need them.

The hero who overcomes his own fears to challenge death, steadfast to a code of honour, duty, and courage, appears throughout Hemingway's later fiction. This code-hero or tutor usually stands as a model to a character such as Jake Barnes who aspires to the same ideal of behaviour, but whose mind is divided and whom temptations beset. The code of the bull-fight, brought to life during the fiesta when quotidian customs such as the exchange of material value are meaningless, is juxtaposed to Jake's 'philosophy' in Paris, and Romero to the parody code-hero Count Mippipopolous.

As Cohn's unfailing absurdity is one aspect of how Hemingway has transformed the pattern we have explored in earlier chapters, Romero's triumph is another. He is a hero unlike any we have encountered so far. Jake, who will model his own heroism in part on Romero's, spies in the boy no hint of irresolvable paradox. Unlike the romantic heroes, Romero's character is singularly integral. He succeeds, utterly, where the flawed romantic yearnings of Kurtz and Jim and Dowell and Gatsby and Robert Cohn are baffled by themselves and by a society fallen from innocence and grace. Many of Romero's impulses are the same as theirs – and he fulfils them. An artist as much as a hero, a priest as much as either, through courage and skill and some indefinable essence of spirit he imposes his will on the world within the ring, this circle of eternity, and dominates his fate.

No small measure of his success is due, of course, to land and heritage – both are ancient and yet primitive, and innocent in a way post-war Paris can no longer be. Romero is the glory of the land and its servant; he must challenge death, let the blood of the bull flow, so that the life of the land and its people are renewed. Though he possesses a dignified, nearly serene detachment when surrounded by others, 'standing, straight and handsome and altogether by himself, alone in the room with the hangers-on' (p. 163), he is never isolated or cut off as the romantic heroes have been.

Romero is the yet unwounded Fisher-King. He has conquered the fear of death, transformed it into art and passion. But he has yet to feel either the horn of the bull or the bitterness of life. Thus, one essential aspect of his tradition he cannot yet fully represent: that the code is of greater significance than the hero. Indeed, a recognition that darkness and death *will* come, met nobly perhaps but not delayed, makes unyielding faithfulness an even greater achievement. Another matador plays that role, if only briefly, and embodies for Jake an attitude of what I have called general irony. For Belmonte, a great matador of his time, has tasted defeat as Romero has not. His presence recalls the older waiter of 'A Clean, Well-Lighted Place' and Manuel Garcia of 'The Undefeated', and anticipates the heroism of Anselmo in *For Whom the Bell Tolls* or Santiago in *The Old Man and the Sea*. They fight the good fight for its own sake and, though the darkness of final defeat lies not far beyond, for their own inwardly derived dignity. Belmonte performs despite pain, humiliation, and scorn.

> Romero did always, smoothly, calmly, and beautifully, what he, Belmonte, could only bring himself to do now sometimes. The crowd felt it, even the people from Biarritz, even the American ambassador saw it, finally. It was a competition that Belmonte would not enter because it would lead only to a bad horn wound or death. Belmonte was no longer well enough. He no longer had his greatest moments in the bull-ring. He was not sure that there were any great moments. Things were not the same and now life only came in flashes.   (p. 215)

Belmonte of course is only a slight figure in the novel, a foil to Romero's brilliance while also a hint of what greatness will come to.

Mark Spilka contends that 'Pedro is the real hero of the parable, the final moral touchstone, the man whose code gives meaning to a world where love and religion are defunct, where the proofs of manhood are difficult and scarce, and where every man must learn to define his own moral conditions and then live up to them.'[8] While it is true that he takes Cohn's place and is the sole unqualified hero of the central tale, the story, finally, is not Romero's but Jake's. And what Jake learns from this tutor, shaping his own more circumscribed heroism out of defeat and bearing his new role and the tale back to the modern world, is the novel's true concern.

VI

Arranging the affair between Brett and Romero, Jake betrays himself and the only positive values left him – those founded on his *aficion*. No other of our narrators has fallen so far or failed himself so totally. From this spiritual nadir, similar to Marlow's feverish brush with death in *Heart of Darkness*, Jake must climb towards a new moral identity.

That exposing a boy as gifted as Romero to a source of corruption is wrong is explicitly established when the American ambassador requests that Montoya send the boy to the Grand Hotel. Montoya seeks Jake's advice, as an American and as an *aficionado*, and Barnes immediately responds, 'Don't give Romero the message' (p. 172).

> 'Look,' said Montoya. 'People take a boy like that. They don't know what he's worth. They don't know what he means. Any foreigner can flatter him. They start this Grand Hotel business, and in one year they're through.'

That same night, however, Brett demands far more than had the ambassador. Having put Jake through the catechism of confirming his love for her, she asks that he pander her to Romero. This will no longer be simple passivity in the face of Brett's profligacy. She bids Jake, *because he loves her*, to serve her up to another man. In doing so he will not only abandon the last vestige of dignity, but will violate the source of his remaining values: the responsibility he bears as an *aficionado*.

Brett knows full well that what she intends is wrong. But because she's a 'goner' (p. 183) and 'can't help it', she wants Jake to understand and condone. Repeatedly he tells her not to do it, that she 'oughtn't'. For all his terseness, his ironic tone, and his sullenness, however, he never addresses the issue of what *he* should do, never hesitates or refuses. In describing the start of the fiesta Jake has claimed that everything 'became quite unreal finally and it seemed as though nothing could have any consequences' (p. 154). As he and Brett set off in search of Romero, at least the immediate consequences must surely be all too clear.

The confusion of narrative sequence in the climactic scenes of the novel approximates Jake's own disorientation. It further heightens the nightmarish atmosphere. One of the most apparent differences between *The Sun Also Rises* and the other novels we have examined is its generally tight correlation of discourse to story. Jake usually relates events essentially in the same order as they occurred. He rarely juxtaposes scenes, events, or characters outside of chronological sequence, as Marlow does, for example, throughout *Lord Jim*. Ironic juxtaposition certainly is present, as we shall discuss at the end of this chapter, but Jake leaves it to the reader to discover appropriate comparisons. The confusion of sequence in these climactic scenes is therefore especially striking.

In chronological order, Cohn knocks out Jake, trails Brett and Romero to the matador's room, returns to his own where Jake finds him, shakes hands, and leaves. By the next morning Cohn has disappeared, and that afternoon Romero kills the bull Bocanegra. As Jake recounts the story, however, we follow him through hours of pain and disorientation. He tells us of the death of Vicente Girones, gored by Bocanegra, and of how Romero dispatches the bull the following day. But this last is a narrative leap forward in time.

> [Bocanegra's] ear was cut by popular acclamation and given to Pedro Romero, who, in turn, gave it to Brett, who wrapped it in a handkerchief belonging to myself, and left both ear and hand-kerchief, along with a number of Muratti cigarette-stubs, shoved far back in the drawer of the bed-table that stood beside her bed in the Hotel Montoya in Pamplona.   (p. 199)

This is more than a brilliantly ironic cameo of Brett's character, her relationship with Jake, and her sensitivity to such trophies.

Foreknowledge heightens the reader's awareness of dramatic irony as the narrative retreats to reveal Cohn's attack on Romero, and heightens, in turn, appreciation of Romero's full triumph when his killing of Bocanegra is recapitulated in detail.

When Cohn discovers what has happened he strikes out. He refuses to be another of the eunuchs in Brett's menage such as Mike Campbell who soddens himself with liquor or Jake who observes, disapproves, and abets nevertheless. Although a parody of the bull-fight, Cohn's pummelling of Mike and Jake is the catastrophe towards which all the group's tensions have been gathering, just as Romero's performance in the bull-ring is the central catastrophe of the fiesta. Romero brings renewal; Cohn tears all masks from the raw truth. Romero will be Jake's tutor, a model of dignity, self-control, and faithfulness to the code. But first Jake's double, Robert Cohn, has had to awaken him to the self-deceiving truths and ignominy of the past.

Even so, Cohn's 'niceness' undercuts the effect of his actions; he lies weeping on his bed, insisting on shaking Jake's hand and, we learn later, he has tried to do the same, to play the noble adversary, with Romero. But Romero won't make a game of it; he strikes Cohn in the face. Even in what is surely his finest moment, a moment of potential redemption, absurdity dogs Cohn.

Cohn's fists have felled Jake; but the real damage comes of the indictment as a pimp. The physical battering reinforces the inescapable truth of the charge and makes further self-deceit impossible. Jake staggers away from the cafe, the world transformed.

> Walking across the square to the hotel everything looked new and changed. I had never seen the trees before. I had never seen the flagpoles before, nor the front of the theatre. It was all different.   (p. 192)

In normal life, character and custom make sense of chaos, create an illusion of continuity and meaningful pattern. But Jake's character of wilful blindness has been shorn clean. We may recall Gatsby awakening from his dream to find 'what a grotesque thing a rose is and how raw the sunlight was upon the scarcely created grass'.

After the fight, Jake seeks a 'deep, hot bath, to lie back in' (p. 193). The impulse has a double root: to find womb-like shelter and to cleanse himself of ignominy.

I could not find the bathroom. After a while I found it. There
was a deep stone tub. I turned on the taps and the water would
not run. I sat down on the edge of the bath-tub.   (p. 195)

After such betrayal, however, Pamplona can provide no shelter,
and purgation will come only after the fiesta has run its course.

Romero begins to act the tutor to Jake in his own response to
Cohn's assault. *His* integrity survives. The reminders of the beating
are only physical, a bruised and swollen face, a sore body. His spirit
triumphs in the ring the next day, overcoming lingering pain.
Because he discovers within himself the potent source of skill and
courage, and expresses it in terms of the code, when Romero
presents his art as a testament to his love, the act achieves the sort of
human meaning that, for Hemingway, matters and endures.

> Everything of which he could control the locality he did in front of
> her all that afternoon. Never once did he look up. He made it
> stronger that way, and did it for himself, too, as well as for her.
> Because he did not look up to ask if it pleased he did it all for
> himself inside, and it strengthened him, and yet he did it for her,
> too. But he did not do it for her at any loss to himself. He gained by
> it all through the afternoon.   (p. 216)

Just as the catastrophe of the evening before gave Cohn the
opportunity to recover enough of himself to fight and depart, and
Jake the chance to confront himself honestly, so the physical beating
Romero suffered allows him to transcend his past performance,
overcoming by force of will and spirit the limitations his body would
impose. He is the greater for it. Instead of being lamed by Cohn or
corrupted by Brett, the boy seizes raw experience and translates it into
his art. He handles Brett with as much dexterity as he does the bulls.

VII

To satisfy his desire for cleansing, Jake travels after the fiesta to the
sea at San Sebastian. That decision, moreover, represents a
courageous choice not to retreat into the hollow safety of what his
life had been before the crisis. It marks Jake's intention to follow the

path begun in Pamplona towards new self-awareness, acceptance of what he has done and, ultimately, to the role of narrator and hero. Returning to France, he travels as far as Bayonne to see Bill Gorton off, and there Jake imagines a stay in San Sebastian; the tone of convalescence is a stark contrast to the recent fiesta.

It would be quiet in San Sebastian. The season does not open there until August. I could get a good hotel room and read and swim. There was a fine beach there. There were wonderful trees along the promenade above the beach, and there were many children sent down with their nurses before the season opened. In the evening there would be band concerts under the trees across from the Cafe Marinas. I could sit in the Marinas and listen.

(p. 232)

San Sebastian means a return to Spain, however, and Bayonne has its own attractions: it offers Jake his old, sheltered relations with the world, the chance to adopt once again his philosophy of value-exchange and thereby to repudiate the painful lessons of the disaster in Pamplona.

Spirit and *aficion* play no role in dealing with the French. With the money he spends, Jake can ensure that he is well liked, having to offer up nothing of himself. Human relations in Bayonne are clear, safe, unthreatening. No laying-on of hands is needed for initiation, only the passing of coin.

You can never tell whether a Spanish waiter will thank you. Everything is on such a clear financial basis in France. It is the simplest country to live in. No one makes things complicated by becoming your friend for any obscure reason. If you want people to like you you have only to spend a little money.   (p. 233)

A return to San Sebastian offers a clear moral choice, a rejection of what has been his life in Paris. But the actual alternative to be discovered there remains uncertain. Nevertheless, although he feels 'a fool to be going back into Spain' (p. 233), Jake leaves Bayonne the next morning.

His brief stay in San Sebastian is an interlude similar to the fishing trip to Burguete. The tone and detail of his swims recall his description of the earlier fishing. Here again is ritual: the cleansing release of past life, the baptism of new.

> I swam out, trying to swim through the rollers, but having to dive sometimes. Then in the quiet water I turned and floated. Floating I saw only the sky, and felt the drop and lift of the swells. I swam back to the surf and coasted in, face down, on a big roller, then turned and swam, trying to keep in the trough and not have a wave break over me. It made me tired, swimming in the trough, and I turned and swam out to the raft. The water was buoyant and cold. It felt as though you could never sink.   (pp. 237–8)

Yet despite the latent significance of these passages, San Sebastian is partly unsatisfying for the reader, if not for Jake. Purgation comes too easily. Jake leaps for the water and past sins slip from him like superficial grime; we find little evidence of meaningful internal struggle. The cleansing merely ratifies a moral decision already made when Jake returned to Spain from Bayonne.

Nevertheless, after the bathing a second crucial choice suddenly arises, as if only now made possible: and it is a following through, a fulfilment of the first. Having returned to San Sebastian, Jake chooses to cut his visit short. He travels farther into Spain to rescue Brett. The trip to San Sebastian purged him clean; as he assumes responsibility for Brett Ashley, Jake's new moral identity at last reveals itself. This is not the same sort of responsibility that Nick Carraway accepted for Gatsby – a gesture of solidarity – but an admission of Jake's own culpability, a willingness to see the act through to completion without self-deception, and a gesture towards emotional freedom.

Jake demonstrates a caustic honesty towards himself after responding to Brett's urgent telegrams.

> That seemed to handle it. That was it. Send a girl off with one man. Introduce her to another to go off with him. Now go and bring her back. And sign the wire with love. That was it all right.
>   (p. 239)

The bitterness is part of the exorcism of past self-delusion: the judgment an explicit acknowledgment that Cohn's charge of pimping was accurate. Jake accepts the truth so that he can accept, in turn, responsibility for it by bringing Brett back. This is no preparation for beginning the cycle of his old life anew, but a necessary summing-up or balancing of accounts to bring that life to a close. The concluding scene of the novel dramatizes the same point: Brett clinging to Jake in the Madrid taxi for solace and protection, trying to resurrect the old phantom of what-might-have-been, the foundation of their relationship. '"Oh, Jake," Brett said, "we could have had such a damned good time together"' (p. 247). But Jake refuses the comfortable illusion. He may well still love Brett. He has come to retrieve her from Madrid, partly because he is responsible for her being there. But he at last acknowledges that the what-might-have-been is a meaningless, enslaving fiction. '"Yes," I said. "Isn't it pretty to think so."'

VIII

The taxi ride in Madrid juxtaposed to the one earlier in Paris not only certifies Jake's moral education; it reveals the structural principle of his narrative. And that principle, in turn, is a further reflection of the way in which he has come to see the world. Places, events, and characters resonate in ironic constellations. Jake rarely makes these relations explicit, however. He demands that the reader share in his education through the course of the tale and recognize for himself the relations between Paris and Pamplona, Count Mippipopolous and Romero, bicycle racing and bull-fighting. Robert Cohn, Pedro Romero, and Jake Barnes themselves stand in a triad of similarities and contradictions which, in a novel of relatively simple outline, creates an extraordinarily suggestive richness.

What emerges is a sensibility, a perspective of general irony informing the many juxtapositions within *The Sun Also Rises*. Light and darkness, faith in human endeavour and an awareness of encroaching *nada*, courage and absurdity, everywhere penetrate the narrative – these have become the governing terms in which Jake understands his experience and recreates the world. This does *not* mean, however, that one opposed element is 'good', the other 'bad'. Each may well further embody the dilemma of general irony. Cohn himself is perhaps the best example. His romantic quest for meaning, his heroic impulses, are as genuine as the absurdity that undermines them. Rarely does life's crucible forge unalloyed character; even Romero may one day be a Belmonte, his greatness forfeited by fighting only bulls with short horns.

Jake cannot remain in Spain, a land fertile enough to succour Romero's heroism, but not the dwelling place for a man who can never again be wholeheartedly innocent, for whom the primitive may renew and teach but not be shelter for long. He must return with Brett to Paris; that is his world. His physical laming, like the modern temper to which it has been an objective correlative, remains uncured. Yet Jake now possesses a complement to his wound: he can act, affirming the lesson learned from experience and tutor, that through art meaning may be re-established, though darkness threatens just beyond the light of such endeavour. Jake is a modern hero because he bears some of that light to a Paris shrouded in sickness, self-deception, and relations based on the premeditated exchange of goods and desires. His tale yokes the fragmentary images of modern experience into meaningful form. We may compare this with Bruce L. Grenberg's comments on Pedro Romero's heroism in the bullring.

> In his firmness and grace, in his most controlled and stylized killing of Bocanegra, Romero provides for Jake an ideal exemplum of man's capacity for creating meaning through art out of the very elements of radical disorder.[9]

Pedro Romero, a true hero and model of manly behaviour, replaces the failed romantic, Robert Cohn. Having recognized the ironic relation between Cohn and Romero – that as different as they are, they share similar impulses – Jake's heroic responsibility is not to eulogize Cohn but to translate something of Romero's art and code to a fallen world.

The pattern we have followed, of narrators assuming and refashioning the fallen mantle from their romantic heroes, begins in *The Sun Also Rises* to evolve, to spin away towards new possibilities for later authors. The pattern changes largely because the world has changed. A central dynamic of the novels we have examined is the narrator's discovery of the illusions of conventional beliefs and of the hypocrisy of modern society. Each narrator has had to discover a new foundation for moral character, one fashioned on an ironic detachment that remains sceptical of any effort towards enduring significance and yet steadfastly affirms the struggle itself. But already in Jake Barnes's Paris — 'everybody's sick' – disillusionment is a general condition. And so, for later novels such as *Absalom, Absalom!* and *All the King's Men* which adopt a familiar structure of earth-bound narrator(s) and romantic hero, a coherent thread through *Heart of Darkness, Lord Jim, The Good Soldier, The Great Gatsby,* and *The Sun Also Rises* will have been tied off. The narrator in this next generation must confront a world reared in irony. To the extent that that is true, Marlow's voice in the darkness, and Dowell's, Carraway's, and Barnes's, will have succeeded in their heroic task.

Notes

CHAPTER 1: *HEART OF DARKNESS*

1. Joseph Conrad, 'Heart of Darkness', in *Youth and Two Other Stories, The Complete Works*, Kent Edition (Garden City, N.Y.: Doubleday, Page & Co., 1926) p. 97. All further page references appear in the text.
2. This term belongs to the brilliant analysis of irony in D. C. Muecke, *The Compass of Irony* (London: Methuen, 1969).
3. Søren Kierkegaard, *Fear and Trembling*, trans. Walter Lowrie (Princeton University Press, 1968) p. 30.
4. Joseph Conrad, *The Nigger of the 'Narcissus'*, Kent Edition (Garden City: Doubleday, Page & Co., 1926) p. 25. All further page references appear in the text.
5. Michael Levenson, *A Genealogy of Modernism: a Study of English Literary Doctrine 1908–1922* (London: Cambridge University Press, 1984) p. 10.
6. Joseph Conrad, 'Youth', in *Youth and Two Other Stories*, p. 3. All further page references appear in the text.
7. Ian Watt, *Conrad in the Nineteenth Century* (Berkeley: University of California Press, 1979) p. 164.
8. Joseph Conrad, *Nostromo*, Kent Edition (Garden City: Doubleday, Page & Co., 1926) p. 521.
9. This term is taken from W. J. Harvey, *Character and the Novel* (Ithaca, NY: Cornell University Press, 1965).
10. For a full discussion of this process see Wayne C. Booth, *A Rhetoric of Irony* (University of Chicago Press, 1974) esp. p. 28.
11. David Thorburn, *Conrad's Romanticism* (New Haven, Conn.: Yale University Press, 1974) p. 124.
12. Walter L. Reed, *Meditations on the Hero* (New Haven, Conn.: Yale University Press, 1974) p. 63.
13. The term is taken from Søren Kierkegaard, *The Concept of Irony*, trans. L. M. Capel (New York: Harper & Row, 1966).

    [T]he whole of existence has become alien to the ironic subject, ... he in turn has become estranged from existence, and ... because actuality has lost its validity for him, so he, too, is to a certain extent no longer actual. (p. 276)

14. Joseph Conrad, *Under Western Eyes*, Kent Edition (Garden City, N.Y.: Doubleday, Page & Co., 1926) p. 279.
15. C. B. Cox, *Joseph Conrad: the Modern Imagination* (London: Dent, 1974) p. 57.

CHAPTER 2: HEROISM AND NARRATIVE FORM IN *LORD JIM*

1. Joseph Conrad, *Lord Jim*, Canterbury Edition (New York: Double-day, Page & Co., 1924) p. 224. Further page references in text.
2. Much of the discussion of narrative form is influenced – though not without significant qualification – by Joseph Frank, *The Widening Gyre* (New Brunswick, N.J.: Rutgers University Press, 1963). Albert Guerard mentions the spatial form of *Lord Jim* within a larger discussion of the form of *Nostromo* in *Conrad the Novelist* (Cambridge: Harvard University Press, 1958) p. 210.
3. Anthony Winner, *Characters in the Twilight: Hardy, Zola and Chekov* (Charlottesville: University Press of Virginia, 1981).
4. Joseph Conrad, Introduction to *Lord Jim*.
5. Ian Watt, *Conrad in the Nineteenth Century* (Berkeley: University of California Press, 1979) p. 278.
6. Paul Bruss, *Conrad's Early Sea Fiction: the Novelist as Navigator* (Lewisburg: Bucknell University Press, 1979).
7. Guerard, *Conrad the Novelist*.
8. David Thorburn, *Conrad's Romanticism* (New Haven, Conn.: Yale University Press, 1974) p. 130.

CHAPTER 3: WATCHING THE ORCHARDS ROBBED

1. Ford Madox Ford, *The Good Soldier: a Tale of Passion* (New York: Random House, 1955) p. 12. Further page references appear in the text.
2. Mark Schorer, 'The Good Soldier: an Interpretation', in Richard A. Cassell (ed.), *Ford Madox Ford: Modern Judgments* (London: Macmillan Press, 1972).
3. John G. Hessler, 'Dowell and *The Good Soldier*: the Narrator Re-Examined', *The Journal of Narrative Technique*, 9 (spring 1979) p. 115.
4. Samuel Hynes, 'The Epistemology of *The Good Soldier*', in *Ford Madox Ford: Modern Judgments*, p. 98.
5. John A. Meixner, *Ford Madox Ford's Novels* (Minneapolis: University of Minnesota Press, 1962) p. 168.
6. Paul B. Armstrong, 'The Epistemology of *The Good Soldier*: a Phenomenological Reconsideration,' *Criticism*, 22 (1980).
7. Armstrong, p. 232.
8. Armstrong, p. 237.
9. Ernest Becker, *The Denial of Death* (New York: The Free Press, 1973) p. 74.
10. Anthony Winner, *Characters in the Twilight: Hardy, Zola, and Chekov* (Charlottesville: University Press of Virgina, 1981) p. 25.
11. Norman Leer, *The Limited Hero in the Novels of Ford Madox Ford* (East Lansing: Michigan State University Press, 1966).
12. Leer, p. 5.

13. Ford Madox Ford, *A Call: the Tale of Two Passions* (London: Chatto & Windus, 1910) p. 290.
14. Leer, p. 47.
15. Schorer, p. 68.
16. Ford Madox Ford, *An English Girl* (London: Methuen & Co., 1907) p. 54. Further page references appear in the text.
17. Søren Kierkegaard, *The Concept of Irony*, Lee M. Capel, trans. (New York: Harper & Row, 1966).
18. Ford Madox Ford, *Parade's End* (New York: Alfred Knopf, 1978) p. 629, Ford's ellipsis.
19. See Thomas Moser, *The Life in the Fiction of Ford Madox Ford* (Princeton University Press, 1980).
20. Cf. Joseph Conrad, 'Preface' to *The Nigger of the 'Narcissus'* (Garden City, NY: Doubleday, Page & Co., 1926) p. xiv. 'My task which I am trying to achieve is, by the power of the written word to make you hear, to make you feel – it is, before all, to make you *see*. That – and no more, and it is everything.'
21. Leer, p. 71.
22. Hynes, p. 101.

CHAPTER 4: WITHIN AND WITHOUT: NICK CARRAWAY

1.   F. Scott Fitzgerald, *The Great Gatsby* (New York: Charles Scribner's Sons, 1925) p. 36. Further page references appear in the text.
2.   See Jerome Thale, 'The Narrator as Hero', *Twentieth Century Literature*, III, 2, (July 1957).
3.   Arthur Mizener, *The Far Side of Paradise* (Boston: Houghton Mifflin, 1965).
4.   See Thale, and Robert W. Stallman, 'Conrad and *The Great Gatsby*', *Twentieth Century Literature*, I (April 1955).
5.   See Gary J. Scrimgeour, 'Against *The Great Gatsby*', *Twentieth Century Interpretations of The Great Gatsby*, Ernest Lockridge (ed.) (Englewood Cliffs, N.J.: Prentice Hall, 1968).
6.   Thomas Hanzo, 'The Theme and the Narrator of The Great Gatsby', *The Great Gatsby: a Study*, Frederick J. Hoffman (ed.) (New York: Charles Scribner's Sons, 1962) p. 289.
7.   Mizener, *The Far Side of Paradise*, p. 74.
8.   F. Scott Fitzgerald, 'The Sensible Thing', *The Fitzgerald Reader*, p. 100.
9.   F. Scott Fitzgerald, *This Side of Paradise* (New York: Charles Scribner's Sons, 1920) p. 239.
10. Ford Madox Ford, *The Good Soldier* (New York: Random House, 1954) p. 115.
11. Marius Bewley, *The Eccentric Design: Form in the Classic American Novel* (New York: Columbia University Press, 1963) p. 277.
12. W. J. Harvey, 'Theme and Texture in *The Great Gatsby*', *Twentieth Century Interpretations of The Great Gatsby*, p. 99.
13. In *The Great Gatsby* only 'in Carraway's interpretation is the fullness of

Gatsby's dream recovered'. David L. Minter, *The Interpreted Design as a Structural Principle in American Prose* (New Haven: Yale University Press, 1969) p. 186. See also, Walter L. Reed, *Meditations on the Hero* (New Haven, Conn.: Yale University Press, 1974).

14. F. Scott Fitzgerald, 'Winter Dreams', *The Fitzgerald Reader*, p. 58.
15. Bewley, p. 271.
16. 'Gatsby's taste in language is as flashy and overblown as his taste in cars or clothes: when he talks about his feelings to Nick Carraway, the words he uses retain echoes from many cheap and vulgar styles. ... Gatsby's feelings for Daisy, the moment he tries to define them, become the banal stereotypes of romantic magazine fiction, and so it is fitting that the language he uses should be vitiated by worn-out images and sentimental cliches.' (Brian Way, *F. Scott Fitzgerald and the Art of Social Fiction* [London: Edward Arnold, 1980] p. 105.

CHAPTER 5: *THE SUN ALSO RISES*

1. Ernest Hemingway, *The Sun Also Rises* (New York: Charles Scribner's Sons, 1926) p. 102. All future page references included in text.
2. Carlos Baker, *Ernest Hemingway: a Life Story* (New York: Charles Scribner's Sons, 1969) p. 135.
3. Arthur Mizener and Philip Young find little evidence of change. Mizener argues that 'when the novel ends, Jake and Brett are exactly where they were at the start. It cannot even be said that they understand their situation better or are better reconciled to it' (Arthur Mizener, *Twelve Great American Novels* [New York: New American Library, 1967] p. 130. Young makes the point from a reader's perspective: 'Constant activity has brought us along with such pleasant, gentle insistence that not until the end do we realize that we have not been taken in, exactly, but taken nowhere; and that, finally, is the point' (Philip Young, *Ernest Hemingway: a Reconsideration* [University Park: Penn State University Press, 1966] pp. 86–7.
4. Early readers latched on to Gertrude Stein's second-hand verdict on a 'lost generation', thereby justifying a primarily dark or satirical reading. Hemingway, annoyed that the phrase snatched out of context had acquired the same *ad hoc* authority as Fitzgerald's 'Jazz Age', insisted in a letter to Max Perkins that the rather oblique fragment from Ecclesiastes was much the more important, and that his novel was not intended as 'a hollow or bitter satire but a damn tragedy with the earth abiding forever as the hero' (Carlos Baker, *Hemingway: the Writer As Artist* [Princeton University Press, 1972] p. 179).
5. Ernest Hemingway, *A Farewell to Arms* (New York: Charles Scribner's Sons, 1929) p. 310.
6. Baker, *Hemingway: the Writer As Artist*, p. 56.
7. Earl Rovit, *Ernest Hemingway* (Boston: Twayne, 1963) p. 55.

8. Mark Spilka, 'The Death of Love in *The Sun Also Rises*', *Hemingway: A Collection of Critical Essays*, Robert P. Weeks (ed.) (Englewood Cliffs, N.J.: Prentice-Hall, 1962) p. 138.

9. Bruce L. Grenberg, 'The Design of Heroism in *The Sun Also Rises*', *Fitzgerald–Hemingway Annual* (Washington: NCR, 1971) p. 284.

Index

Armstrong, Paul, 53

Baker, Carlos, 92, 94
Becker, Ernest, 54
Bewley, Marius, 80, 86
Booth, Wayne C., 18
Bruss, Paul, 34

Conrad, Joseph
  Heart of Darkness, 12–27
  Lord Jim, 28–48
  The Nigger of the 'Narcissus', 4–7
  Nostromo, 16–41
  Under Western Eyes, 22
  'Youth', 8–12
Cox, C. B., 23

Eliot, T. S.,
  The Waste Land, 93

Fitzgerald, F. Scott
  Tender is the Night, 80–1
  The Great Gatsby, 72–91
  'The Sensible Thing', 75
  This Side of Paradise, 75–6
  'Winter Dreams', 84–5
Ford, Ford Madox
  A Call, 56–7
  An English Girl, 57–8
  The Good Soldier, 49–71
  Parade's End, 61–2
Frank, Joseph, 28

Grenberg, Bruce L., 116
Guerard, Albert, 28, 45

Hanzo, Thomas, 73
Harvey, W. G., 16, 82

Hemingway, Ernest
  'A Clean Well-Lighted Place', 94
  Nick Adams stories, 95
  A Farewell to Arms, 94
  For Whom the Bell Tolls, 108
  The Old Man and the Sea, 108
  The Sun Also Rises, 92–117
Hessler, John G., 49
Hynes, Samuel, 51, 70

Kierkegaard, Søren, 3, 14–15, 22, 61

Leer, Norman, 55, 57, 69
Levenson, Michael, 7

Meixner, John A., 52
Minter, David L., 83
Mizener, Arthur, 72, 74, 93
Moser, Thomas, 64
Muecke, D. C., 1

Reed, Walter L., 22, 83
Rovit, Earl, 95

Sartre, Jean-Paul, 14–15
Schorer, Mark, 49, 57
Scrimgeour, Gary. J., 73
Spilka, Mark, 109
Stallman, Robert W., 73

Thale, Jerome, 72, 73
Thorburn, David, 18, 48

Watt, Ian, 15
Way, Brian, 86
Winner, Anthony, 30, 54

Young, Philip, 93